Managing People and Employee Relations

INTRODUCING THE SERIES

Management Action Guides consists of a series of books written in an Open Learning style which are designed to be

■   user friendly

■   job related

Open Learning text is written in language which is easy to understand and avoids the use of jargon that is usually a feature of management studies. The text is interactive and is interspersed with Action Point questions to encourage the reader to apply the ideas from the text to their own particular situation at work. Space has been left after each Action Point question where responses can be written.

The Management Action Guides series will appeal to people who are already employed in a supervisory or managerial position and are looking to root their practical experience within more formal management studies.

Although Management Action Guides is a series of books that cover all aspects of management education, each book is designed to be free standing and does not assume that the reader has worked through any other book in the series.

Titles in The Management Action Guides series are

Planning and Managing Change

Handling Conflict and Negotiation

Making Effective Presentations

Achieving Goals Through Teamwork

Creating Customer Loyalty

Managing People and Employee Relations

Managing People and Employee Relations

MANCHESTER
O · P · E · N
LEARNING

KOGAN
PAGE

First published in 1992 as *Management in Organisations* by Manchester Open Learning, Lower Hardman Street, Manchester M3 3FP

This edition published in 1993 by Kogan Page Ltd

Kogan Page Limited
120 Pentonville Road
London N1 9JN

© Manchester Open Learning, 1992, 1993.

British Library Cataloguing in Publication Data

A CIP record for this book is available from the British Library.

ISBN 0 7494 1141 4

Printed and bound in Great Britain by Biddles Ltd, Guildford and Kings Lynn

Contents

GENERAL INTRODUCTION

Customers are becoming increasingly important in the lives of most organisations as competition increases. Customers are now presented with more choice than ever before; and this represents a considerable shift of power away from producers to consumers. A number of factors have combined to bring about this change

- **Deregulation**: the withdrawal of controls and privileges which protected a number of industries from effective competition and put other industries under direct government control.

  Privatisation has been only a minor element in this change, although it has been the most visible. In the last decade road transport (both freight and passenger), financial services, air transport, radio broadcasting and telecommunications have all been opened up to competition, with or without privatisation of public corporations. This trend has been common to nearly all developed countries, regardless of the political complexion of their governments

- **Globalisation**: companies are increasingly viewing the whole world as their potential market, and pressing their governments to remove whatever barriers still exist to international trade. Many large companies have, in effect, lost their original national identities and have become completely internationalised. They are managed from a number of different centres, and produce and sell their products anywhere in the world. Competition and choice is coming from more places than ever before

- **Technology**: on the production side, modern technology has been applied in three main areas – in production processes, in the products themselves, and in communication systems. The resulting effects for the consumers have been: an increasing variety of goods to choose from, a steady reduction in the prices of what were traditionally 'luxury goods', and a greater awareness of what is available together with better access to it

- **Rising Standards**: at least for the majority of people in this country, rising real income means that a larger proportion of the income is available for them to use how they choose. Rising standards of living have led people to expect rising standards of quality and service. Typically they want better rather than more

INTRODUCTION: MANAGING HUMAN RESOURCES AND EMPLOYEE RELATIONS

As well as achieving specific work goals through teams, managers are expected to show effectiveness in their day to day management of people - to approach personnel matters and employee relations in such a way as to make the best use of the human resources of the organisation which come within their field of influence. It is inevitable of course that from time to time there will be problems, difficulties and conflicts, particularly in a business environment where change is more frequent and rapid than at any previous time. Foreseeing and dealing with the causes of potential problems wherever possible is obviously desirable; but where grievances or conflicts do arise, knowing how to handle such things in line with company policies and any legal obligations, and in a positive and accountable manner is essential.

This involves awareness, knowledge and skills in many areas. An understanding of the personnel areas which relate to human resource management - recruitment, training and updating, appraisal and development - and of how these are effectively carried out; an awareness of the impact of Trade Union and employment legislation and of how local agreements and procedures affect the manager's approach in employee relations; a knowledge of what good grievance and disciplinary procedures involve, and the skills of handling such problems both at the informal and formal stages; and recognition of the importance of good communications skills for managing employee relations successfully.

It is at these areas we shall look in this book; its **overall aim** is that when you have worked through it, you should have a better appreciation and command of the knowledge and skills required to manage effectively the employee relations and the human resources within your area of work.

1 HUMAN RESOURCES MANAGEMENT AND CHANGE

We live in a business environment where the pressures and forces of all kinds demanding change are greater than they have ever been

■ the political and legal changes occurring with the deregulation and opening up of markets as a result of a single European market with ever increasing competition for the markets

■ the continuous pressures for product and service changes from ongoing technical change and development, and the effects of computer technology and innovation in almost every aspect of industry and life

■ the pressures of customer expectations as they pursue choice, novelty, change and improvement

■ social and economic changes leading to changed patterns of employment, wealth distribution, life-styles and consumption in the UK and in other countries with which we trade

■ economic and political factors such as domestic economic policies, changing patterns of international trade and markets, the globalisation of money markets and exchange rate fluctuations, the revolutionary economic changes in eastern Europe, the price of oil and so on

■ political and social pressures on industry from environmental issues

fig 1.1

All these and many more factors have produced a business environment where accepting the need for continuous improvement and change is a fundamental necessity for survival in most industries.

When thought through, this has profound implications for the way in which companies approach their human resource management and employee relations if they are to prosper in the increasingly competitive marketplace.

The prospect of change will affect people in different ways according to their situation and whether they see the likely outcomes as beneficial to themselves or not. In general terms, even where people see possibilities of advantage, they are likely to feel some degree of apprehension also.

There are many wholly understandable reasons for this

- most change brings **uncertainty** - it is rare for people to be able to forecast or envisage the precise effects of change and in the absence of certainty, people will fear the worst

- even where advantages are promised, people are **losing things** in the exchange - familiar and safe routines, known relationships, known status and influence etc

- having to adapt to new situations and learn new skills may create **anxiety and fear**

- some aspects of the changes may in fact be **deleterious** for them - greater workload, more repetitive, boring work, more supervision etc

Such feelings and fears may well produce passive or active resistance to change and such resistances must be addressed and overcome if change is to be carried through successfully.

We cannot deal comprehensively here with the management of change, but a brief list of things which managers can do to assist the process would include

- make people aware of the reasons why change is needed

- explain why the status quo is unsatisfactory and not in people's best interests in the longer term

- try to envision and communicate what the future will be like after the changes

- listen to and address honestly individuals' concerns

- give all possible information as promptly as possible and do everything possible to prepare for it

But all these things are unlikely to win the commitment and positive motivation of people to take on change if there is not **already present** - in the team and in the organisation as a whole - an approach to human resources and employee relations which **as a matter of course** listens to, respects, communicates with, involves and develops individual employees, and addresses their needs and concerns. The realisation of this has led (as we shall see later in this book) to changing approaches to Industrial Relations in many companies in many parts of the world, with an emphasis on treating **people**, not money or machines as an organisation's most valuable resource. It is seen by them not as window dressing or a temporary fashion, but as **a matter of business efficiency** - the only way to win the motivation and commitment which will enable the organisation to respond continually to the necessity for change.

To be trusted and to be effective, such an approach needs to show itself in every aspect of human resource management and development - in the operation of formal personnel activities like training and appraisal, grievance and disciplinary procedures, in the formal negotiation of work conditions and rewards and in the informal day to day running of affairs within an organisational team.

It is with the managerial role in these areas and the knowledge and skills needed to implement such an approach that the rest of this part of the book will be concerned.

CHAPTER SUMMARY

Having completed this chapter, you should now

■ accept the need for continuous improvement and change in order for a company to survive

■ realise the importance of overcoming resistance to change by listening to and addressing the individuals' concerns

If you are uncertain about any of these areas, look back and re-read the relevant parts of the text.

2 GETTING THE RIGHT PEOPLE

How personnel matters such as recruitment and training, personal appraisal and development, disciplinary matters and grievances etc are dealt with, will vary of course from organisation to organisation but managers will be involved to a greater or lesser degree, informally and formally, personally or in liaison with others, in all these areas. And getting the right people and making effective use of them is the first essential if the needs of the organisation are to be met properly.

In this chapter we will examine

- recruitment and selection procedures
- effective interviews

Recruitment and Selection Procedures

Recruitment and selection of people whose abilities and potential match the demands of particular jobs involves eight processes

- analysing the job requirement
- describing the job
- describing the person you are looking for
- advertising the job
- drawing up a shortlist
- preparing for the interview
- conducting the interview
- making the final decision

ACTION POINT 1

In which of these areas might managers be involved in your company and in what ways? If you are unsure, check out your company procedures for notifying and filling vacancies.

Assuming that you do not work in a specialist Personnel Department (and depending on your particular company procedures), a manager's role and involvement are likely to centre around

■ discussion or decisions about whether a job vacancy needs to be filled and how

■ notification of vacancies to Personnel, discussion of the job description and the person specification to be used

■ consultation or decisions over shortlisting for interview

■ conducting or taking part in the actual selection interview

Is This the Job We Need?

New markets, reorganisations, a new product range or service, new technology may all create additional jobs or replacements for existing jobs and where this happens, thought will obviously be given to what kinds of new jobs are needed. When a member of staff leaves, however, there is a tendency to automatically notify Personnel to get the replacement procedure underway.

Job needs can change and when someone leaves it should be thought of as a good opportunity to think carefully about the current and future needs of the section that they worked in. Rapid change is constantly demanding new working practices and skills, while others are made redundant (or more demanding) by the introduction of new technology. A function which was once only one of many responsibilities attached to a job may now call for a specialist. So before notifying a vacancy three questions should be addressed

■ do we really need to replace the person who is leaving?

■ has the job changed since it was last advertised?

■ would any modification of job roles or creation of a different job help the section perform better?

The Job Analysis and Job Description

Once it's been decided that a new job is needed or that a lost staff member should be replaced, a job analysis should be completed or checked. This process is often a group undertaking, involving a person who has done the job, that person's manager and a personnel specialist.

In most large organisations all graded jobs have job descriptions in existence held by the Personnel Department, arrived at after analysis of

- the job's main purpose and the context in which it exists
- the scope, the responsibilities and the accountabilities involved
- the tasks and skills involved
- the physical and mental demands of the job
- the working conditions

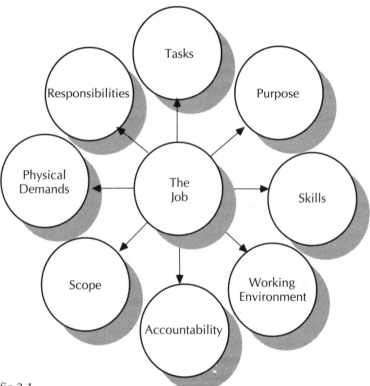

fig 2.1

This provides the job description content which should identify precisely the **purpose, duties and relationships** of the job.

An example of a job description set out in a commonly used format follows

Job Title	Personal Assistant to the Marketing Manager (Grade AO2)
Reports to	The Marketing Manager
Responsible for	Five clerical workers in the Marketing Manager's office
Main Objectives	To provide administrative support to the Marketing Manager; to deputise when necessary; to supervise the work of clerical staff in he department
Main Duties	To process external correspondence, internal mail and other documents; to supervise the work of clerical staff in this area
	To ensure the confidentiality of all correspondence and to handle matters not requiring the Marketing Manager's immediate attention
	To take minutes at meetings as required
	To supervise the typing, reprographic work, records maintenance and other duties of clerical staff
	To receive company visitors
	To undertake from time to time any further duties that may be considered in keeping with the job designation
Physical Conditions	The job holder will occupy a workstation within an open-plan office shared with five clerical workers. The office is situated in the company's modern, purpose-built premises in Uxbridge
Conditions of Service	35 hour week - Monday to Friday, 9.00 am to 5.00 pm, 1 hour lunch break. Five weeks annual leave. Salary £11,250 - £14,750 starting point dependent on experience and qualifications

ACTION POINT 2

Using the sample job description given on the previous page as a model, and without consulting any job description you may already have, write one for your own job.

If you have a written job description, compare it with what you have written and consider the reasons for any differences between the two.

Describing the Person

All too often, employers make expensive mistakes in selecting staff because they have only a hazy idea of the sort of person they are looking for. Drawing up a profile of the 'ideal' candidate or **person specification** helps avoid this pitfall and it is the logical progression from analysing and describing the job. Managers may well be asked for their views in this area by Managers or Personnel, so it is important to know what makes for a good person specification.

ACTION POINT 3

What characteristics do you think a good job specification would have?

The main characteristic of any good job specification would be that the qualities sought from the ideal applicant would span **the demands of the job** and would **all be related clearly to those demands.**

A second important characteristic is that **it should not discriminate** unfairly, directly or indirectly, intentionally or unintentionally, against any groups of candidates. This applies not simply from legal considerations (as on grounds of sex or race), but because it is foolish to miss potentially suitable candidates by applying some criteria which are **irrelevant to good performance** of the job.

Where the person specification satisfies these criteria, it becomes a valuable tool in the selection process, since it helps us to

■ determine exactly what we are looking for in applicants

■ assess each candidate in relation to the ideal profile

■ assess the candidates in relation to each other on an 'equal' basis

A Simple Person Specification Model

There is no standard way of setting out a Person Specification, but the model below offers a simple means of structuring one. It suggests 3 headings under which employers can list their requirements, and can be used to structure an advertisement, shortlist, and later the selection interview itself.

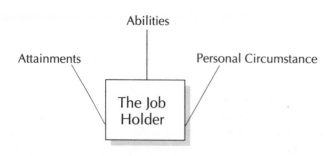

What are the requirements ?

fig 2.2

Abilities - these refer to qualities which can be demonstrated, mainly at interview; but the application itself might indicate some, such as written communication. The **level** of the ability needs to be shown also eg. 'To manage a section of 15 clerical staff'; 'To write monthly productivity reports for non-technical staff'.

This would also include an assessment of the level of general intelligence that a person needs to do the job properly.

Attainments - these should be directly related to facts and minimum entry requirements that are appropriate to the job. eg General Education: a degree in Civil Engineering; Professional & Vocational Training: Membership of the British Institute of Management etc. Experience both in and out of paid employment would also be relevant.

Personal Circumstances - this is an opportunity to check and test for an individual's commitment to the company, their ability to work unsocial hours, to work a rostered shift pattern etc.

It will be helpful for selection purposes to identify also which qualities or qualifications are **essential**, so that a person will not be employed without them - and which ones are merely **desirable** (that is, other qualities could compensate for their absence or they could be developed later through training etc).

Shortlisting

This is the next stage in which managers will be directly involved after Personnel have carried out the advertising and despatch of application form processes.

When Personnel, using the **person specification**, have identified those candidates who

■   meet many or most of the requirements

■   meet some requirements and could, with training, meet more of them

they may consult the departmental manager about a final shortlist of people to interview for the job (and possibly a reserve list also).

Effective Interviews

Managers may well be involved at this stage in the interviewing itself and possibly in the preparatory arrangements too. The conduct of job interviews varies considerably, according to the type of post being filled and the preferences or procedures of the employer or company. Some interviews are extremely formal and candidates are examined by a panel of interviewers. Others are one-to-one discussions conducted in a much more relaxed atmosphere.

But in whatever way they are conducted, they have a specific aim: to assess the suitability of each candidate for the job on offer. **Careful planning** will help achieve this purpose. It involves making decisions about

■   when to interview and for how long

■   who will conduct the interview

■   where to interview

■   how to receive candidates

■   what questions to ask candidates

The **interview date** will depend on how long is needed to complete each stage of the recruitment phase and the availability of the people interviewing.

The length of time for each interview will depend on the level and type of post to be filled. But sufficient time must be allowed to ask all questions, to give candidates time to answer and 'make their case', to probe their responses where necessary and to answer any questions they may have. It must also allow time for a proper assessment of each candidate between appointments. (Trying to assess all the people interviewed in one final 'reviewing session' will not do justice to them or make a good assessment, even if notes were made during the interviews.)

Proper arrangements should be made for receiving and welcoming candidates with somewhere candidates can sit before their interviews. The interview location should be **free from interruption** and comfortable in terms of **seating, ventilation and heating**, and attention should be given to the arrangement of furniture in the interview room which will influence the interview atmosphere. For instance, a desk between interviewer and interviewee creates a psychological barrier, so that the atmosphere tends to be more formal than if they sit alongside each other. A large office desk acts not only as a physical barrier, but also a psychological one.

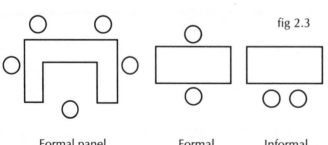

fig 2.3

Formal panel interview

Formal one-to-one interview

Informal one-to-one interview

Whether it is a panel interview or a one-to-one interview questions need to be carefully prepared for all the work that has gone into the selection procedure to be effective; and if it is a **panel interview**, all the interviewers should discuss in advance what they are going to ask candidates and who will ask each question.

Asking the Right Questions

In preparing, an interviewer should always

■ look again at candidates' application forms for information that may need checking or clarifying

■ re-read the person specification and job description to focus their ideas for questions

It is important then to ask **the right kinds of question** to make use of the interview time and the information they already have. There are four main types of questions an interviewer can use

■ closed questions

■ open questions

■ probing questions

■ problem-centred questions

Closed Questions

A closed question is one which requires a 'Yes' or 'No' answer, or which does no more than establish a single fact. It does not invite the candidate to express their ideas or feelings, except in the most general and abbreviated terms. Examples of closed questions would be

'Where did you take this course?'

'Did you see it in the Staff Vacancy Notices?'

'Did you get any book-keeping experience there?'

'How long have you been in Information Management?'

Closed questions are useful if you just want to check information, but they won't encourage candidates to reveal much about themselves. As the name implies, the answers tend to 'close off' the exchange, unless another question immediately follows.

Open Questions

Open questions on the other hand are worded in such a way as to produce a full and revealing reply from the person being interviewed

'What were your duties in that job?'

'What do you see yourself doing in five years time?'

Open questions encourage an interviewee to open up about themselves and give them an opportunity to show the interviewer(s) what they are like and why they would be suited to the job on offer. They also give the interviewer a much **better opportunity to assess** the candidate's personality, motivation, 'depth' and general suitability, because, with open questions, the amount of talking an interviewer must do is reduced, and time to listen carefully and to weigh up the candidate is increased.

Probing Questions

A probing question seeks to learn **more** about something a candidate has already said

'Exactly why did you decide to leave your last job?'

'You say you're in charge of the stock control system. Could you describe how this system works?'

Such questions test the genuineness of the applicant and the depth of consideration they have given to things, but they also give the opportunity for the candidate to show their quality more fully as they enlarge on their earlier statements.

Problem-centred Questions

Problem-centred questions are designed to assess the candidate's likely response to particular situations, to see how they would deal with the particular problems which they might meet in the job

'If you were the manager here, how would you deal with a member of staff who was obstructive and resented your being appointed from outside the company?'

ACTION POINT 4

Look back over this section and for each type of question discussed, formulate two examples of your own.

Listening, Summarising, Note-taking

At the beginning and end of an interview when giving candidates information and answering their questions, the interviewer will take a predominant part. But in a good interview it is the candidate who will do most of the talking, primed and focused by the questions and by the **non-verbal feedback** given by the **active listening** of the interviewer.

Showing readiness to listen in your posture; looking in an interested, non threatening way at candidates; encouraging or indicating understanding by nods and appropriate facial expressions - these things will help the candidate show themselves at their best and help direct the interview also, giving signals to the person about when they have said enough on a topic, where they need to expand and so on.

The ability to reflect on what the interviewee has said and then, briefly and accurately, to **summarise** it from time to time, is also a skill worth cultivating. It ensures facts and understanding are correct and gives the opportunity to rectify omissions or clarify things before going on to other questions as this example shows

Interviewer: So, you left school in 1984 and joined Watson's as a trainee mechanic. Then you took a course in motor vehicle maintenance before returning to Watson's as a skilled mechanic. Is that correct?

Candidate: Well, actually, I never left Watson's. They sent me to college on day-release and when I'd finished the course, I was promoted.

Note-taking is also essential where several people are being interviewed but this should be done as unobtrusively as possible so as not to interrupt the flow of the interview or put off the candidate.

One way of doing this is to use an **interview assessment form**. Ticking off answers on a form enables an interviewer to record impressions of candidates and at the same time listen attentively to what they are saying. The assessment form as its name implies will also be the basis for making the selection decision after the interviews are completed. We will look at an example later.

Conducting the Interview

Most candidates feel rather nervous at the beginning of an interview. For this reason the interviewer should spend a short time putting a candidate at ease and establishing the **rapport** which will relax them to allow a frank and detailed discussion to take place. A few informal conversational questions after greeting them can help - 'It's a good way in from Sutton, Mr Peters. Did it take you long to get here?'

The interviewer should also **let candidates know what to expect** by outlining the sequence of the interview at the beginning, which will also reduce anxiety and help discussion flow more smoothly.

Once the main body of the interview is underway, the interviewer must be sure to ask all their prepared questions, **listen** actively to the candidate and **observe** their body language, summarise and record important points, and be ready to probe further where necessary. A **chronological** approach is often taken to the middle stage of the interview working through details of the candidate's education or early career up to the present.

When the interview has brought out the information needed to assess a candidate properly, it can be brought to a close, by indicating this to the candidate, giving an opportunity for them to put any questions they may have, and answering these as fully and frankly as possible. It's in the interests of both company and candidate that a person who takes up a job knows exactly what is involved.

Finally, the interviewer should let the candidate know what will happen next by saying, for example, something like this

'Well, Mr Peters, thank you for answering all my questions so fully. As neither of us has any further questions, let me outline what will happen next. I expect to make a decision by the end of the week and I'll write to you early next week. Then, if you're successful, I'll ask you to write back to say whether you accept the job. Is all that quite clear and acceptable?'

ACTION POINT 5

Imagine you alone are interviewing a candidate shortlisted for a job (supervisory or otherwise) in a department or section of your own company.

Set out your **preparations** for the interview, describe how you would **conduct** it and give details of the **questions** you would ask.

Then check your answers against the chapter you have just been studying.

Making the Decision

As we noted earlier, at the end of each interview and **before** the next candidate is seen, the interviewer or panel should reflect on what has happened and if they are using a **candidate assessment form** add to it any further notes or gradings they wish to. An example of such a form follows.

Applicant Assessment Form

Grade applicants on the following scale

A   Highly suitable for the post

B   Suitable

C   Suitable with further training

D   Unsuitable

Job title...................................

Applicant's name...................................

	A	B	C	D comments
Abilities				
Attainments				
Personal circumstances				

The basis for using the form will of course be the person specification that was drawn up earlier. By entering under the headings the specific requirements of the job in each area, the interviewer can see how far each candidate's performance matches the abilities, attainments and personal circumstances required by the job. (For example, under 'Abilities' you could put 'Clear verbal expression'; under 'Attainments' you might say 'Minimum HND in Electronic Engineering'; and so on).

Preparation of this beforehand will allow the interviewer to concentrate in the interview on bringing out and probing the candidate, **ticking off** a grade in each area once satisfied that enough has been brought out for them to make a sound assessment.

Candidate assessment forms provide a fair and straightforward method of comparing candidates with each other in relevant standardised and relevant areas, unswayed by 'instinct', or first impressions, or even looks.

Making the Offer

The successful candidate will often be offered the job verbally (subject to satisfactory references if these have not yet been taken up) at the conclusion of the selection process. Since good candidates do sometimes decide a job is not for them after interview, this means an offer of the job can be made to any other suitable candidate if the first choice declines. Finally, after any references have been checked, a formal letter with full details of the terms and conditions of the post will be sent by Personnel for the candidate's acceptance.

ACTION POINT 6

Look at the recruitment and selection procedures within your company, and compare them with what you have read in the book. Assess and explain the reasons for any differences you find.

CHAPTER SUMMARY

Having completed this chapter, you should now

■ understand the processes involved in recruiting and selecting people whose abilities and potential match the demands of the job

■ appreciate the need to assess the ways in which a job description might change

■ know how to plan and carry out effective interviews

If you are uncertain about any of these areas, look back and re-read the relevant parts of the text.

3 MAKING THE MOST OF PEOPLE

Having recruited the best people available, human resource management demands that the best use is made of them. And to do this requires continuous **appraisal, development and training** of people by managers in relation to the collective and individual objectives and standards that are continually being set.

This in turn demands systematic auditing and monitoring of performance, the **revision of standards** and the use of **training, coaching and counselling** to correct performance wherever it is possible for improvements to be made.

Management of performance should be a **continuous and dynamic cycle.** Traditional appraisal systems often tend to simply look backwards over a six or 12 month period; effective performance management seeks to look forward, to review progress, to appraise the team individually and collectively against a measured standard of excellent performance, to identify where improvement can be made and obstacles to it, and to train and develop on a continuing basis, resetting targets and maintaining a constant flow of information.

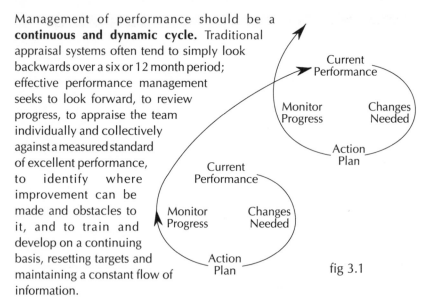

fig 3.1

CHAPTER SUMMARY

Having completed this chapter, you should now

■   realise the importance of making the best use of people via continuous appraisal, development and training

4 TRAINING FOR DEVELOPMENT

We have just suggested that training should be a regular and **on-going process**, but there are also particular times in each person's career development when a manager needs to ensure that **specific essential training** is received, for example

- induction training for newcomers

- basic job skills training for newly promoted staff or updating of skills for longer serving staff

- development training when change occurs in systems, equipment or even style of management

- training for a new job level or different responsibilities - in supervisory or managerial skills, for example

In the bigger company it is likely that there will be special training courses arranged through Personnel in many of these cases. If so, they will have been arrived at by an analysis of the knowledge, skills and behaviours required in the trainee's new situation and then the drawing up of a programme to meet those training needs. And where managers are responsible for

- training new team members

- ongoing development of individual and team performance by training

the approach to effective training will be based on the same principles.

ACTION POINT 7

What do you see as the essential stages in planning and carrying out effective training?

You will probably identify four essential elements

- analysing what knowledge and skills and attitudes are required to do a job well

- assessing current performance in those areas and deciding on any changes needed

- preparing a training action plan

- monitoring progress and appraising results

Identifying the Needs

An analysis of each job into its constituent **tasks** and **activities** will provide the basis for

- identifying the knowledge, skills and attitudes needed to do a job well

- agreeing standards of performance in those areas which will lead to satisfactory results

These standards in turn will allow us to assess the standard of a person's current

- knowledge

- skills

- attitudes

and will identify where there are gaps to be bridged between current achievement and the ideal level for the job

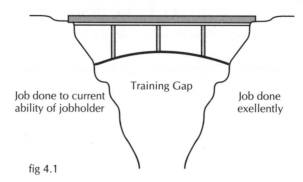

Job done to current
ability of jobholder

Training Gap

Job done
exellently

fig 4.1

Tasks and Activities
As a simple example, consider the job of a sales assistant.

The sales assistant's **tasks** as shown in the job description might include

- welcoming customers
- offering and demonstrating goods
- selling goods
- accepting payment
- keeping records
- arranging displays of goods

Each of these tasks will involve **activities**. For example, arranging the display of goods might include

- checking the counter display each morning
- setting up special offers prominently
- pricing and labelling goods
- liaising with designers over selection of central display material

Knowledge, Skills and Attitudes

The tasks and activities of a job will be carried out poorly, adequately or excellently according to the jobholder's **attitudes, knowledge and skills**. So the next stage in assessing training needs is, as we just noted, to decide what these will need to include for the job to be done well.

Knowledge of the product(s) being sold might include such things as

- quality
- colour, size, range
- price, credit terms, discount
- availability, delivery
- how to use it or them
- benefits to be gained from making the purchase

Skills might include

Sales and social skill

- greeting people and making them feel welcome
- answering questions quickly and positively

- understanding and satisfying customers' needs
- closing the sale

Money and paperwork skills

- taking money and giving change
- handling cheques, credit cards, invoices, receipts etc
- operating electronic tills and calculators
- working with codes and numbers

Display and demonstration skills

- arranging goods on display
- handling goods without soiling or damaging them
- demonstrating them efficiently
- pricing and labelling accurately and tidily

Attitudes might include being positive, polite, helpful etc to the customer and being co-operative and loyal to colleagues

Setting Standards, Assessing Current Performance

The next stage in analysing training needs is to look at each task and activity and identify where the knowledge, skills and attitudes needed are best demonstrated - that is, **where the best results are achieved** in each task or activity, and to decide

- whether the jobholder matches up to this standard of outcomes and performance
- whether training is the answer and if so, what kind

By assessing **individual** training needs in this way the manager will produce the basis for a comprehensive and ongoing **team training programme**, for after considering all the tasks and activities of the team, a detailed picture will emerge of any 'gaps' or possible improvement areas.

Using a Matrix Checklist

Where a manager has a team of people doing the same job, or performing easily comparable tasks and activities, one way to produce this detailed picture of team performance is to use **a matrix checklist** with graded standards of performance or marks noted down for each skill or activity. The following example illustrates how such a checklist is constructed.

JOB - SALES

SYSTEMS & PRODUCT SKILLS

JOB TASKS	Correct Procedure	Sales/ Inquiry Ratio	Add-on Sales
STAFF NAMES			
Chris	7	7	3
Tracy	9	6	3
Frank	2	7	4

CUSTOMER CARE SKILLS

	Courteous Helpful	Prompt Answer	Product Knowledge
Chris	3	2	2
Tracy	8	7	2
Frank	9	6	8

Such a matrix would need to include **all** the tasks and major activities of each job in order to get an accurate picture and the first step in marking up the assessments is to put a maximum grading against an excellent operator before assessing the performance of the rest of the team against that level of excellence.

So the routine for completing your matrix would be

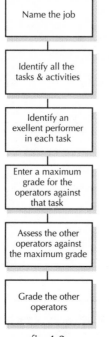

fig 4.2

Of course, it is possible to create performance assessment 'scores' for people doing quite individual jobs based on a 'notional standard' of excellent performance, but it is important that this should be a realistic and agreed standard based on results which could be achieved.

ACTION POINT 8

1   If you are in a managerial or supervisory position with a team of people doing the same or comparable jobs, following this step by step routine, prepare a matrix of all the tasks and major activities necessary to do that job excellently. (A current job description may be available to give you the initial information you need).

2   Identify someone who performs to a maximum standard in each task or activity. By comparing the way the others work give them each a personal grading.

(If you are not in this situation, prepare a checklist for your own job and assess your own performance against a notional standard of the best possible results in each area - one which takes realistic account of the job constraints)

Preparing a Training Action Plan

At this point it is necessary to decide whether training is the answer to any performance improvement needs. Training is not the only way to bridge the gap - other actions may be needed, for example, a re-organisation of the workload to iron out peaks and troughs. It may be necessary to discuss this with managers and colleagues. But where training would help, the next step would be to define training objectives, select the best methods to achieve these and prepare a training plan. Another simple analysis mechanism can help here.

Using a Training Needs Schedule

A **Training Needs Schedule** lists those tasks and activities where the score is less than maximum and identifies what is needed to reach that standard. This might be more knowledge, greater skills, better motivation, more confidence and so on.

As is apparent from the example, a Training Needs Schedule can also incorporate basic ideas about how and when the training needs are to be met, but for an effective Training Action Plan, the proposals need discussing and agreeing with the team member (and anyone else involved) in more detail before it is put into operation.

Staff Member:	Tracy			
Task	**Competence**	**Help**	**From Whom**	**When**
Procedures	Very good - a model staff member in this regard	None needed		
Sales/enquiry ratio	Adequate - but could improve with help and encouragement	More confidence and assertiveness	Initially counselling and feedback. Outside course if needed. Follow up monitoring by supervisor	Stage 1 immediately Stage 2 after a 3 month review
Add-on	Poor - needs development	More product knowledge needed plus confidence (as above)	In-house training course on product material. Personnel to organise. Follow-up monitoring by supervisor	As soon as possible. Next round of product training if possible

---

ACTION POINT 9

What would you consider necessary in a Training Action Plan?

The plan needs sufficient detail for use later in monitoring progress. It will involve setting targets for improvement with specific results to be seen from the training, giving such things as

- ■ an accurate description of each required change wherever possible in measurable terms

- ■ the timescale in which each change is to be made, with start and finish dates

- ■ the type of training and who must take the **action** to see through the change

- ■ how and when progress will be checked - by performance review over a period, by informal report back from the trainer and trainee etc.

Monitoring Progress

We shall be looking at progress or appraisal reviews as a way of monitoring both the performance and the training and development of people a little later in this book. But such a formal review may be some time away and it is desirable to check at the time on whether a training programme is meeting its objectives by informal observation, feedback and discussion.

Training Methods

Choosing the type of training method will obviously depend on the training needs identified in any individual situation. Where a change of technology or methods is impending, a company training course or one arranged through an outside training agency might be appropriate; for work improvement of an individual a targeted coaching programme on the job might answer the need; team training sessions might be the solution where a manager identifies common weaknesses across a whole group; a newly appointed manager might attend a management skills course at a local college or study by supported Open Learning; and so on. In selecting training methods, managers need to consider the extent to which their training objectives can be met and what support can be provided on or off the job to back up the training programme.

ACTION POINT 10

1 Using for your format the example given on page 34, complete a Training Needs Schedule for the staff member Frank referred to in the matrix checklist on page 32.

2 Refer to the matrix that you prepared under Action Point 8 and work out a training Needs Schedule for one of your team members identified there.

CHAPTER SUMMARY

Having completed this chapter, you should now

■   understand how to identify gaps to be bridged between current achievement and the ideal level for the job

■   know how to use a matrix checklist to grade standards of performance of each skill or activity by a particular person and a training needs schedule for improvement

If you are uncertain about any of these areas, look back and re-read the relevant parts of the text.

5 SKILLS DEVELOPMENT THROUGH COACHING

Coaching is a specialised training technique taking place in the workplace and aimed at encouraging specific **skills development.** Where skills 'gaps' - whether technical or related to behaviours - are identified by a training needs exercise, or by staff experiencing problems, coaching should be considered. For success it demands

■ good communication skills in the coach

■ a systematic plan for skills improvement using a step-by-step approach.

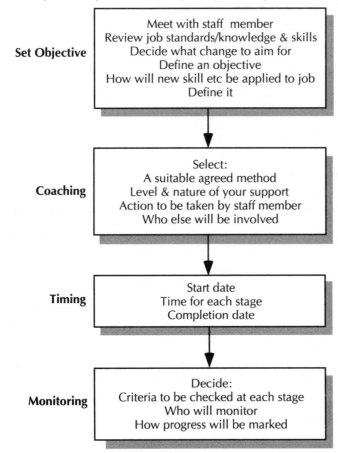

Set Objective
Meet with staff member
Review job standards/knowledge & skills
Decide what change to aim for
Define an objective
How will new skill etc be applied to job
Define it

Coaching
Select:
A suitable agreed method
Level & nature of your support
Action to be taken by staff member
Who else will be involved

Timing
Start date
Time for each stage
Completion date

Monitoring
Decide:
Criteria to be checked at each stage
Who will monitor
How progress will be marked

fig 5.1

A Step-by-Step Coaching Plan

Having identified the specific coaching need (by review of the job standards and the skills required), the manager and team member should together agree

■ clearly defined target outcomes for change as a result of the coaching

■ a suitable coaching method, who else will be involved and what support the manager can arrange to be given

■ a written plan of what this will involve for the team member

    (a)   Attend a demonstration on...

    (b)   Talk to the people at...

    (c)   Work with and observe...

    (d)   Practise the activity on...

    (f)   Report back on progress..

■ a timescale for the coaching sessions with reasonable urgency over completion, since the sooner the objective is reached, the sooner the morale boost of success is achieved

■ the criteria to be used to measure success, who will monitor progress, at what intervals and how

Basic Coaching Technique

The technique of coaching itself primarily involves demonstration, communication, and observation of practice. Whoever is coaching should

■ explain clearly the new skill which is the subject of this particular coaching session or the nature of the performance problem which needs correction (and why it is important), then say how this will be covered in the coaching session and what the desired outcome will be

■ demonstrate the necessary actions in manageable stages, at the same time describing what they are doing carefully, so that the person fully understands and can master the activity

■ check that the activity has been understood and mastered, by getting the person(s) to carry out the complete activity under observation

■ give the person(s) the opportunity to practise the activity (preferably there and then), to reinforce what has been learned

ACTION POINT 11

Summarise briefly the essential elements of a coaching plan. Then check your answer with the section just studied.

CHAPTER SUMMARY

Having completed this chapter, you should now

■ understand the need to encourage the development of specific skills

■ understand the essential elements of a coaching plan

If you are uncertain about any of these areas, look back and re-read the relevant parts of the text.

6 DEVELOPMENT THROUGH COUNSELLING

There are many areas of work where specific training or coaching is not appropriate to overcome problems or attitudes or bring about improved performance, but where listening, discussion, support and possibly advice will be a more suitable approach.

Counselling (which includes that **developmental feedback** we have looked at earlier) is an important tool of work improvement as well as a means of developing both individual team members and a successful and well motivated team. It is a process of helping your team to see their objectives more clearly, of getting them to acknowledge and identify obstacles to good performance, of developing their abilities to work through problems themselves and to come up with their own solutions.

A manager who is a successful counsellor will avoid spending too much time solving problems for the team or fire-fighting, but instead will develop a team in which responsible initiative makes use of the team's full resources to constantly improve performance.

What is Involved ?

Counselling will usually arise when either the manager or the team member becomes aware of some problem which is standing in the way of the best performance of the job. Under time and work pressure, it is all too easy for managers to

- simply give their solution when asked for help
- give directives and instructions when they spot a problem

The aim of counselling is to **help someone to help themselves** (which may also involve bringing them to the point of **wanting** to change some work behaviour so as to improve their performance).

Suggesting a solution may be necessary at some point, but it is not the most important counselling skill. **Listening** probably is.

A patient and well directed exploration of the problem with pertinent but open and concerned questions, undertaken in a receptive and positive way, which concentrates on the **performance difficulties** and on **finding a solution** (not on the individuals involved who may feel defensive or under pressure on some point) is the basis for successful counselling. It should also aim to get team members to suggest their own solutions, which will give them the motive and commitment for future action.

It will involve

■ an individual exchange of ideas about how to correct matters and decide jointly the best course of action

■ considering if the task structure or the resources and tools available need changing to make effective performance possible

■ providing any necessary corrective instruction, training, coaching or support

Handling Work Improvement or Problem Solving Counselling

In the counselling feedback exchange, if the team member has not drawn attention to the problem themselves, the manager will need to show their awareness of it, concern about its work effect and readiness to help in finding a solution. It should not be done in a personally critical way which will raise resentment or resistance, but as positive and helpful feedback about performance.

The key points of the counselling discussion will be to

■ agree on the problem

■ work out a realistic plan

■ establish progress checks

■ summarise what has been agreed

The climate needs to be established as being receptive and supportive at the outset. A good way to set the theme of the meeting but to show confidence that improvement will be made and that their contributions to help solve the problem are being sought is to use the **'Theme and Cue'** procedure.

(1) The **'Theme'** establishes the subject of the meeting, so that the individual recognises that there is a problem, understands clearly what the desired performance is and knows in what way current performance does not meet the need. Often the person will accept the problem immediately or may even have brought your attention to it, but where a team member doesn't immediately see

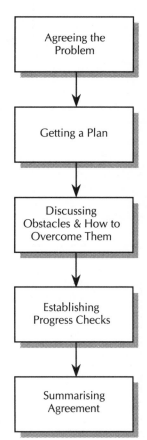

fig 6.1

the problem or the need for improvement, some discussion or elaboration may be needed that points out the possible consequences of continuing to operate in this way -

> 'Roy, I'd like to talk to you about completing the invoicing paperwork. Accounts tell me you completed the C209s wrongly three times last month and, as you know, we could face penalties from Excise if the return's not right...'

(2) The **'Cue'** which follows is an open question that seeks a solution to the problem, or action that the individual can take which will remedy the situation.

> 'How do you think you can/What do you think you can do to ensure the figures are correct in future?'

(3) The person should then be encouraged to **analyse the problem** themselves at this point and to **develop an action plan** to overcome it - by asking further probing questions to establish the precise difficulty. Any **possible problems** the remedial plan might run into need considering, as well as any **support** or change required to help them perform more effectively.

(4) The next essential step is to **establish progress checks** to let the person know that the situation will be monitored to see if the agreed plan of action is working.

(5) Finally what has been agreed should be **summarised** clearly and commitments confirmed about taking the agreed actions to solve the problem.

ACTION POINT 12

What do you see now as the potential advantages of counselling as a technique of work improvement (for both supervisor and team member)?

By approaching work problems generally in this way and by encouraging team members to come up with their own solutions, the manager will

- ensure that effective action is taken to maintain and improve performance
- gain greater commitment to the solutions
- give their people a greater sense of personal responsibility
- encourage them to 'own' their own problems
- increase their confidence and sense of personal contribution
- build stronger personal and team relationships by working alongside team members to improve work performance

The team member with a problem gains help to

- see more clearly what is really needed
- express anxieties or tensions surrounding the problem which may prevent a clear view of the issues
- resolve problems more skilfully
- be readier to take responsibility for solution of work difficulties in future

---

ACTION POINT 13

Imagine that a team member puts their head around your door at the end of the day saying, 'Have you got a minute? I've got a problem with the introduction of this new computerised paperwork system.'

Following the suggested routine, work out some questions you would ask or statements you might make under each heading to encourage the team member to find a solution for themselves.

Listening

Clarifying

Summarising

Probing

Identifying

Reviewing Options

Recommending

Instructing

CHAPTER SUMMARY

Having completed this chapter, you should now

■ understand the importance of counselling as a work improvement tool and a means of developing a successful and well motivated team

■ realise the need to encourage people to help themselves

If you are uncertain about any of these areas look back and re-read the relevant parts of the text.

7 PERFORMANCE APPRAISAL AND DEVELOPMENT

The central part played by review and appraisal procedures in effective management of human resources will be very clear by now. They are integral to achieving work tasks through objectives, to the development of individuals in work teams, and to all kinds of work improvement programmes through training, coaching and counselling. As we noted earlier, the conventional appraisal interview has tended to be a formal, once-a-year, backward looking review of performance, often associated simply with bonus payments, or salary increases, or criticism of past performance instead of the forward looking, positive process it should be.

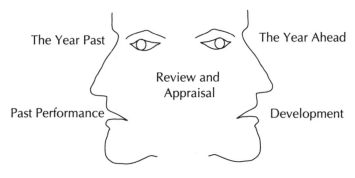

The Year Past

The Year Ahead

Review and Appraisal

Past Performance

Development

fig 7.1

Good performance review and appraisal looks in two directions

■ it reviews past performance and checks it against the goals aimed at in key areas; it identifies what has been accomplished and assesses progress

■ it also recognises failures or problems or areas for improvement; and looks to future development in relation both to specific goals and to the future training and development of the individual concerned

It is realistic, however, to recognise that initially people may not feel wholly positive about performance reviews. They may be anxious that they will be found wanting in some respect. And where there are problem areas, some managers also may prefer not to have to formally assess another person's performance.

However, where

- ■ manager and team member speak informally about performance as a matter of course throughout the year, with credit given for good work and developmental feedback given helpfully

- ■ open, positive communication is the norm in the team

- ■ there is proper briefing of team members so that they know the procedures and can prepare for the review and make positive use of it

then such anxieties and negative feelings should be avoided.

Preparing for Review

The first thing that managers should make clear in arranging an appraisal review with a team member is that the meeting will look forward as well as back, and that it is an opportunity for the person to give some thought to how they would like to see things developing for themselves (through training or changes of duties, for example) over the next 12 months (or whatever the review period is).

At this stage it is wise to agree a detailed agenda of what is to be covered in the review, so that the person knows exactly what is involved and when it is to take place. The manager may also suggest that the individual could carry out their own exercise of self-assessment coupled with self-development prior to the appraisal interview. Suggesting this, with some guidelines if wanted (like those given in the next Action Point), will be a positive indication to them of managerial interest in their personal development, as well as in past and future performance.

The manager then needs to gather all information already held or elsewhere available about performance over the review period (including, of course, details of agreed objectives and the actual results achieved). All this needs to be considered carefully and positively and thought given to items for discussion on the agreed agenda.

ACTION POINT 14

To appreciate what is involved for team members undertaking self-assessment, try this yourself. Take a look for six months or a year in either direction and answer the questions that follow.

Your answers to the questions will depend of course on your personal position, but it may be helpful to check out what you have written with one of your immediate superiors.

Reviewing back

How have I developed in my knowledge, skills, team relationships, relationships with other contacts?

What are my major achievements this year in my job, in my personal development?

Looking forward

How would I like to develop my knowledge, skills, team relationships, relationships with other contacts?

What would I like my major achievements to be next year in my job, in my personal development?

What help will I need to achieve these?

Effective Appraisal Interviewing

As with job interviews, successful appraisal reviews should be held in private, comfortable surroundings, with no interruptions from phones or people and with sufficient time for a full exploration of the issues raised. Any appraisal forms to be completed for personnel records should be to hand with all the other papers and records gathered; and seats of equal height at the same side of a desk are more likely to make the individual feel it is a joint exercise for the benefit of all than if there is a 'status difference' in the seating arrangements.

Review is also a **two way activity**, not just an assessment of performance and obtaining agreement to such changes as are necessary; it is also about what help, support and motivation can be given managerially to achieve targets. The most successful performance appraisal reviews are those where both people feel they have made a worthwhile contribution and that there has been an **exchange** of views and information. To achieve this, a manager may have to work to encourage the team member being interviewed to talk freely and openly.

ACTION POINT 15

What do you think are some of the ways in which an interviewer can encourage an open exchange?

The interviewer should

- clearly express a supportive and positive attitude to the person and process, recognising the value of what has been achieved and indicating confidence in continued development

- show by their words, expression, manner, and body language that they are listening to what the team member has to say; giving them space to explain **their** perceptions of what was planned and what was achieved in the review period

- ask genuinely for suggestions and solutions as well as making proposals

---

ACTION POINT 16

Set down as brief points what you would see as the main elements to cover in a performance review.

The main interview should cover

- a detailed review of the job performance and specific key objectives aimed for in the review period, of what was achieved and how it was achieved

- identification of any problem areas or 'bad news', and discussion of how these can be worked through successfully

- identification of what the team member can do to improve performance further in the different job areas

- identification of what the manager can do in terms of training, coaching, counselling and support to enhance future performance

- a review of training progress where appropriate

- agreement of goals and specific standards to be met in the forthcoming review period

- discussion of the person's development aspirations and what the manager can contribute to their achievement

How the Review should be Conducted

In carrying out the review it is important for the manager to

- focus upon performance, behaviour and results rather than on the individual personally

- present their own perceptions of situations as such, not as facts, and seek by open questions, probing and listening to find out whether the team member sees things differently or agrees

- make sure the discussion relates to specific performance standards and criteria, possible improvements and probable results, avoiding vague generalisations and judgements such as 'good' and 'bad'

- avoid mixing together areas where success has been achieved with areas that require critical attention

- use questions to summarise what has been discussed and agreed at each stage of the review, so as to ensure an agreed understanding

'Good News' and 'Bad News'

The appraisal area which managers generally find most difficult is in passing on '**bad news**' - discussing the failure to achieve satisfactory standards, or suggesting that there is some kind of behaviour or style problem which needs to be looked at.

A 'bad news' item in the review should be kept separate from problem-solving discussion (which may be a later stage but will confuse the issue initially). It is best for the interviewer to

- give the specific information or comments simply and factually, keeping it brief but not abrupt, and maintaining eye contact

- allow time for the reaction - anger, denial or excuses may follow and the person may need some space to digest the news before a positive reaction can be developed

- identify the implications for the team member and together work to find a solution to the problem and an action plan to implement it

'**Good news**' is, of course, much easier to deliver. And managers should welcome the motivational opportunity of being able to give clearly focused recognition and praise for targets achieved and team contributions well made.

Winding Up

An appraisal review should always end up with an agreed final summary of the meeting which confirms what has been jointly decided about future objectives, performance improvement, training and development needs, support to be provided, timescales agreed and so on. This should be gone through verbally at the close and then confirmed by written memorandum as part of the record of the meeting.

ACTION POINT 17

List the basic necessary steps in the preparation and carrying out of an effective appraisal interview.

CHAPTER SUMMARY

Having completed this chapter, you should now

■ realise the importance of review and appraisal procedures in effective management of human resources

■ know how to conduct a successful appraisal interview

If you are uncertain about any of these areas, look back and re-read the relevant parts of the text.

8 INFLUENCES UPON EMPLOYER/EMPLOYEE RELATIONS

At the beginning of this book, we noted how the ability to adapt successfully to continual change was a feature of today's industrial and commercial marketplace. We noted too the implications this had for the approach to human resources management and employee relations if a company is to gain the commitment of its workpeople.

Employer/employee relations have two aspects

■ the formal machinery for consultation and negotiation and resolution of problems, with all the agreements and procedures which surround it

■ the informal area of employee relations as they are affected by the day to day activities of the workplace - the organisation of work, the implementation of changes, the resolution of grievances, work problems, discipline issues and so on

The knowledge and skills of managers at the 'sharp end' of handling these issues are very important influences, but there are many other factors also, internal and external to an organisation and many quite outside their control, which will affect both the specifics of employer/employee relations and the general climate in which they operate.

ACTION POINT 18

Note down briefly as many factors as you can think of under two headings - 'External' and 'Internal'.

Internally you might have noted such things as

■ the approach and attitudes shown to human resource and personnel management at every level from the board to the manager and in every aspect of work - from recruitment through training, career and skills development, performance monitoring and appraisal, promotion procedures, discussion and implementation of change, the company communications climate, grievance and disciplinary procedures, the available rewards package and how it is negotiated, the attitudes to employee and customer health and safety issues - all the range of attitudes and behaviour to people dictated by the company culture and values

■ the approach to the rights and expectations of employees in respect of union membership; the relationship between employers and the local TU representatives; the relationships between TUs themselves where employees cover a range of unionised jobs

■ organisational and structural factors affecting conditions of service, available rewards, development opportunities or job satisfaction

Your list of external factors may have included such things as

■ the impact of TU and employment legislation such as the 1980 and 1982 Employments Acts, the 1984 Trade Unions Act, Health and Safety Acts and Regulations or Equal Opportunities legislation

■ the local and national industrial relations climate and that relating to any particular industry

■ social, political and economic factors such as

(i) changed government policies in economic and trades union matters since 1979, with removal of trade union immunities from legal action by employers in some circumstances, and legislation against the 'closed shop'

(ii) increasing competition caused by deregulation of markets, removing of tariffs, high performance of other manufacturing economies like Japan, West Germany etc

(iii) the effects of the recession of the early '80s with its high unemployment levels, intensification of competitive pressures and the drive for business efficiency

(iv) changes in attitudes of and towards Trades Unions

■ the introduction of new technologies (as in the newspaper industry and other areas of the media)

We have already looked at what is needed for effective management and good individual and team relations in several of these areas. And in the chapters which follow we will look at some of these other features which the supervisor and manager will have to take account of if they are to manage employee relations effectively.

CHAPTER SUMMARY

Having completed this chapter, you should now

■ understand the importance of being aware of both internal and external influences, which will affect employer/employee relations

9 A CHANGING CLIMATE

Conventionally and historically, industrial or employer/employee relations in the UK have been described and seen in terms of **'stakeholding' groups** - employers, shareholders, workers - who have basically conflicting interests in the industrial enterprise they are jointly part of, and who co-operate and negotiate, often uneasily, primarily in pursuit of their particular interests and concerns as stakeholders.

Shareholders, particularly institutional ones with very large shareholdings, may 'negotiate' at times management or policy changes (through their financial stake) if they are dissatisfied with investment returns or management policies. More frequently and visibly we see the **employer** and **employee stakeholders** (usually represented by Industrial Relations management teams and Trade Unions) exerting their powers and influence in negotiating matters of interest to both (wage levels, conditions of employment etc) through collective bargaining locally and at national levels.

Another common feature of industrial relations (but declining in recent years) has been the representation of different groups within a company - particularly craft and skilled workers - by several different unions, with rigidly defined job demarcations and hierarchies of status reflected in pay differentials. Even employers who encourage trade union representation for employees as a means to orderly negotiation and reliable agreements, have commonly argued that this leads to inefficient working practices, productivity problems, demarcation disputes and a continuing upward pressure in wage negotiations as groups try to maintain or reduce wage differentials between themselves and others.

These perceptions of employer/employee relations as basically **confrontational** reflect, of course, genuine differences of interest; so it is certain that pressures for change, differences, conflicts and the need for negotiation will remain prime features of industrial relations. But as well as differences of interest, there are some elements of the work enterprise which are of common interest to both parties and over the last decade a number of factors have suggested that some changes of attitude and approach are taking place amongst both employers and trade unions.

ACTION POINT 19

What do you think might be seen as a primary common interest for employers and employees as stakeholders?

Clearly, although there may be disputes about how it is best attained and the balance of interests, the greater the competitive efficiency of a business concern the more likely it is to survive and prosper and to be able (provided it so chooses) to give long term job security and high rewards to the employees.

And many commentators would say that, over the past decade, there have been some indicators that both employers and employees are seeing productive employer/employee relations as stemming from a less confrontational approach - one in which

- employers see the advantages of gaining the goodwill and commitment of their workpeople

- employee representatives see the need for change, and for continuing innovation and competitiveness to ensure continuing business success and security

This does not mean to say, of course, that hard negotiation is not the order of the day in any discussion or dispute, with both sides seeking to get 'the best results' from their own perspective; but it does entail (if carried through) a degree of trust and respect for each other's interests, rights and good faith which should

- make the negotiating process more productive

- focus the energy and ingenuity of the negotiators on finding best solutions rather than on resistance and confrontation

Some Trade Union Responses

Some trades unions (notably the EETPU and to a lesser degree the AEU and the GMPTU) have responded to the new economic and political climate, the problems of unemployment, falls in union membership and increasingly fierce competition in home and world markets by

- amalgamations to form larger unions with consequent reductions in the number of individual unions

- a greater readiness to meet employer demands for flexible work organisation, the breaking down of skills barriers, productivity deals, single union representation and even 'no strike' deals, in return for the right to represent a workforce, to gain enhanced rewards packages and employee status, increased consultation and participation and so on

Influences from other Countries

Such an agreement perhaps also suggests that different **approaches to industrial relations in other countries** may also be having some effect on employer/employee relations in this country.

The **Japanese** company culture with a great emphasis on job security for life and shared benefits from company prosperity, together with comprehensive and ongoing training and skills updating programmes, has meant that the most fertile source of change and innovation in Japanese industry is the workforce itself because they know that they will share in the benefits as well as the pains of change.

Sweden and **West Germany** also both have traditions of strong trade unions which tend to work co-operatively with employers, seeing the long term interests of their members as bound up with the business success of their companies - but with a tradition also of worker representation, information sharing and consultation to a much greater degree on the employers' side.

fig 9.1

It is often argued that such **open communication** and **sharing of information** about the current productivity, costs and profitability of a company, and its future planning and investment needs, make for

- more realistic employee expectations in wages and conditions negotiation

- greater trust and willingness to discuss positively and co-operatively on both sides

- far greater input from the employee side in terms of realistic and innovative suggestions for improvements in performance and productivity

Some Employers' Responses

Amongst some employers there has been an increasing emphasis in recent years on pursuing efficiency, excellence and market place prosperity, not through confrontational methods (although there are still many examples of such an approach to be seen) but by trying to win the commitment of employees to company goals by co-operation, through

- greater openness and fuller consultation

- better company communications both formal and informal

- the sharing of information and decisions at all levels

- a culture which takes a positive approach to employee relations issues both in formal negotiations and in the informal approach of its managerial staff

This seems to reflect the indirect influence again of the **Japanese approach** to winning company loyalty and commitment, as well as the experience of some large **American corporations** expounded in management theory through the influential Harvard Business School.

These companies take the view that their success in a difficult and competitive business climate depends upon their employee relations in the broadest sense; that their greatest resource is their people; and that encouraging and rewarding co-operation, trust and the development of people is more productive in business terms than a confrontational approach. A management approach and style of a similar kind is also seen in a number of successful non-unionised companies (like IBM and Marks and Spencer) who have consciously set out to provide working conditions, rewards packages and management styles sufficiently attractive to make union membership seem 'unnecessary' to their employees.

CHAPTER SUMMARY

Having completed this chapter, you should now

- understand the importance of winning company loyalty and commitment to achieve success.

10 THE SUPERVISOR AND EMPLOYEE RELATIONS

Employee relations in general within any company will be vitally affected, perhaps even determined, by feelings 'on the ground' in individual departments and sections.

Managers may have no influence over the sort of conditions of service issues resolved by formal (and possibly national) negotiation; but in the implementation of agreements or change, in their handling of people's grievances or conflicts, of poor work performance or disciplinary problems, resource difficulties or safety issues - and a hundred other things - they will play a critical part in creating or undermining a positive climate of employee relations. They also have a vital role to play in the interpretation, implementation and communication of company policies and procedures in such areas. To eliminate the causes of all work grievances or conflicts or problems is an ideal we may aspire to, but one which is unlikely ever to be realised fully. Difficulties arising from differing interests, priorities and perceptions are inevitable where people are working together.

In dealing with such daily problems, they will have to take into account a range of factors, both formal and informal, which will affect whether they handle them correctly, effectively and positively.

ACTION POINT 20

What kind of factors will the supervisor or manager need to be aware of and take into account if they are to handle issues of employee relations effectively and positively?

Amongst many factors they will certainly need to be constantly aware of are

- the impact of industrial relations legislation relating to employment, trades unions, equal opportunity and other issues

- employer/employee agreements on such things as conditions of service, work procedures, grievance and disciplinary matters and so on

- company policies and regulations and the need to implement and communicate them

- the need for work resources and the environment which enable individuals and team to do their jobs well

- the desirability of a work climate in which employee relations problems can be anticipated and prevented, or dealt with in a positive, co-operative way

- the need to communicate clearly and appropriately in any situation

- whether an issue is best handled formally or informally and when it may be necessary to move from one kind of action to the other

fig 10.1

ACTION POINT 21

From your work on individual and team motivation, what would you say were the important factors in creating an environment and climate conducive to good performance and employee relations?

Check your answer against the list of team and individual needs noted in the text on Action-centred Leadership in Chapter 5 and Creating the Right Climate in Chapter 6.

CHAPTER SUMMARY

Having completed this chapter, you should now

■ be aware of the importance of creating a positive climate of employee relations

■ have a better awareness of the factors which will affect whether daily problems are handled effectively

If you are uncertain about any of these areas, look back and re-read the relevant parts of the text.

11 FUNCTIONAL COMMUNICATION AND EMPLOYEE RELATIONS

How managers listen and communicate with people is critical in creating the environment in which people can do a good job. It affects relationships within the team and between manager and team. It also allows recognition and defusing of potential trouble informally before serious difficulties develop. And in situations where formal procedures are needed to deal with a problem, it is vital to the proper exploration and resolution of the situation.

Ineffective or inefficient communication leads to inefficient and ineffective performance, as well as to such problems as misunderstandings, distrust, resentments, dissatisfaction and general demotivation.

One useful model which managers may use to plan their communications is called **Functional Communication** in which **the purpose** of the discussion (what we want to accomplish) determines **how we conduct** the discussion.

Kinds of Discussion

Work discussions can be divided into four major categories according to their purposes. These are to

- give information (Announcement)
- get information (Discovery)
- work together to solve a problem (Problem Solving)
- reach an understanding or agreement (Negotiation)

Announcement in its simplest form consists of two steps

- giving the information
- making sure that information has been clearly understood by the other party

When the information is complex or involves many steps, it may be best to break it down into 'chunks' and give it to the other person one piece at a time.

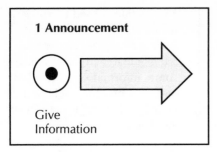

fig 11.1a

Discovery has two basic key steps also

■ getting information from the other party

■ making sure it is complete and accurate

It makes sure that in fact finding, handling grievances or complaints, we get the relevant 'Who', 'What', 'When', 'Where', 'Why' and 'How' of a situation.

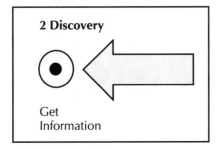

fig 11.1b

Problem Solving differs from Announcement and Discovery in its focus on future actions to be taken. The four key steps are

■ giving the need

■ getting a plan to solve the problem

■ agreeing on progress checks

■ summarising what part each is responsible for

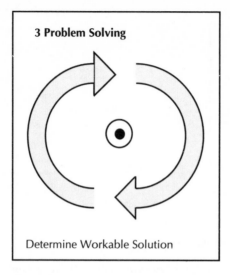

fig 11.1c

Negotiation is used when views differ to reach a mutual understanding or agreement. It requires that each party exchange some information; then both parties work to reach mutual understanding or agreement. Its four key steps are

- giving information
- getting information
- reaching an understanding
- confirming or clarifying

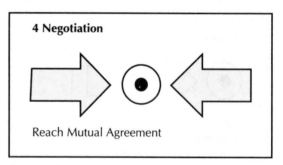

fig 11.1d

These steps are usually repeated more than once to clarify positions and needs until agreement and understanding are assured.

Selecting the Right Form of Discussion

When the wrong form of work discussion is used, the exchange is often confusing or misleading or wrong expectations are raised which then are not satisfied. A manager who uses the problem solving discussion form to tell people about a decision that has already been made, for example, is likely to sound 'phoney'. Such a manager would gain more co-operation and trust by using the announcement form because it is more appropriate to the situation.

ACTION POINT 22

Decide the correct form of discussion for each situation given below

1   Allocating duties to a junior team member

2   Investigating a customer complaint

3   Resolving conflict between two team members

4   Explaining a product change

5   Working out a compromise with a team member

6   Giving feedback

7   Finding out the reasons for a delay in a production schedule

8   Encouraging a team member to plan how they might avoid timekeeping difficulties

Setting the Right Direction - Theme and Cue

The ability to raise a topic that needs discussion - particularly a grievance or disciplinary topic - **without setting up hostile or defensive reactions** from the individual(s) concerned is important if the discussion is to develop on the right lines, free from misunderstandings, resentments and wasteful personal cross currents. Two basic tools to get the discussion rolling in the right direction are **theme statements** and **cue lines.**

The theme statement **identifies the purpose** of the work discussion and briefly sets its limits.

The cue line gets the other person talking and encourages them to **respond directly to the subject** of the statement.

The same theme statement can be the opener for several different forms of discussion, depending on what cue line is used after it.

Example

Theme Statement:

'Peter, some of the tools were not to hand ready for the servicing checks during that last turnaround.'

Cue 1 'What can you tell me about them?' **Discovery**

Cue 2 'What can you do to ensure they are all on place for the next turnaround?' **Problem solving**

Cue 3 'Please check the tools are all ready for use next time. Is that OK?'

Announcement

Notice how the cue lines focus on gaining a specific response from the team member. They avoid mixing up the communication with anything which will make the message ambiguous.

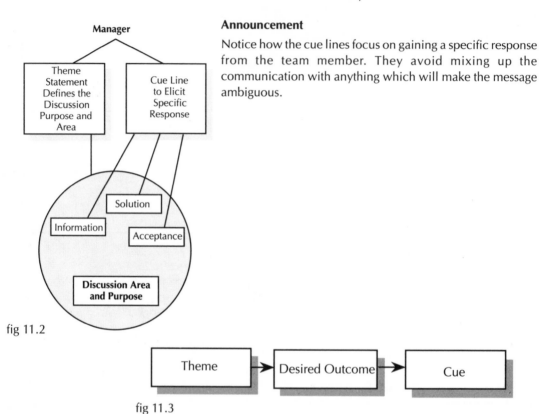

fig 11.2

fig 11.3

ACTION POINT 23

Think of a situation or problem you come across regularly with your team and write down a theme statement and four cue lines - one appropriate to initiate each of the four types of exchange or discussion - Announcement, Discovery, Problem Solving and Negotiation.

For Successful Discussion

There are four essentials for successful discussion of work or employee relations problems, whether the discussion is formal or informal. They are to do with Climate, Priming, Probing and Focusing.

Good Climate

The **Climate** should set the stage for a free and open exchange without communication blocks by establishing the right mood for the exchange.

It can be encouraging and friendly (as in talking through a work assignment for example), or it can be cool and controlled (as in a discipline discussion), but if the discussion is to be fruitful and positive, it is important to **avoid creating a critical, hostile and negative atmosphere** - whatever the type of discussion.

ACTION POINT 24

We have dealt earlier in our discussions of recruitment and appraisal interviews with how a good climate can be created. Note down all the elements you recall.

Priming Tactics

These can be **non verbal**, signalling that we want to hear what people have to say - by leaning forward, eye contact, nodding etc - or **verbal** techniques including

- **tune-ins** or short verbal signals to show attention and encourage the person to continue ('Go on, I want to hear what you have to say...')

- **paraphrasing** what has previously been said to show that it has been heard and understood ('So you feel belittled by Alan always repeating the simplest instructions..')

Probing Tactics

These are useful to ensure information received is accurate and complete and get to the central point of a conversation. They include

- **open questions** which require a detailed, well focused response rather than a simple 'Yes' or 'No' ('OK Jim, can you tell me how it happened?', 'What did you do then?' etc)

- **offering** - that is, supplying alternatives or solutions on how to do something in a way which prompts responses ('Have you considered suggesting an alternative? or 'Have you thought about looking at it in this way....')

- **reconstructing** - to help bring out forgotten information or establish fuller understanding ('So let's try to reconstruct what happened. The materials came a week behind schedule...')

- **testing** - to check accuracy and bring to mind overlooked facts ('You say you did all the routine checks. Did you log them as completed individually at that time?')

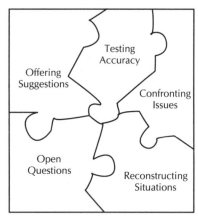

- **confronting** - to bring about acceptance of an issue being evaded or ignored ('I understand what you've said and that you had things on your mind, but you must have left the machine running, mustn't you, for the accident to have happened?')

fig 11.4

Focusing the Discussion

In discussing a potential problem area or grievance, individuals may at any time become unco-operative, side tracked, or emotionally upset. It is important to recognise the side tracks and the feelings - but also not to lose the subject in hand. Maintaining focus is helped by

- dealing with **one thing** at a time

- using **recues** - that is, repeating the original cue line to restate the purpose of the discussion

- **'flagging'** (or noting down for later discussion) of topics raised which need to be discussed, but which, if followed now, will distract from the intended purpose of the present discussion

■ **summarising** to bring the focus back to the main point of the discussion by establishing where you have got to as well as ensuring that any misunderstandings or missed information are picked up on

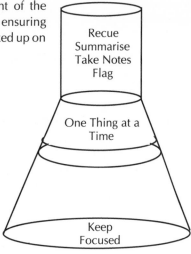

Recue
Summarise
Take Notes
Flag

One Thing at a Time

Keep Focused

fig 11.5

ACTION POINT 25

Read the following, then say briefly which of the focusing techniques you would use to keep the discussion on track.

Theme and Cue

'Peter, some of the tools were not to hand ready for the servicing checks during that last turn around. What can you do to ensure they are all in place for the next turn around?'

Response

'Oh, I'll see that they're all sorted out, but we'd been pushed after the previous turn around. Anyway I don't think the way they're laid out is the best it could be - I know it's what the manual says, but I reckon the layout of the kit really needs re-organising. I was talking to Jim last week and he agrees it could be much better laid out to save time on the servicing. Then we'd have more time anyway to sort them out between turnarounds ...'

Compare your ideas with what follows.

Peter is avoiding the cue to come up with an answer to the immediate problem, except in the most vague terms. Instead he raises another problem not really directly related to what you have asked him as a kind of excuse. You might well 'flag' his suggestion about reorganisation of the tools layout for later discussion, but you will need to 'rescue' him about how he proposes to ensure the tools have been sorted out properly before the next turn around.

Ending a Discussion

Openers set the topic and the direction of any work discussion. Proper closure ensures that the purpose has been, or will be accomplished. It consists of **Summary** and **Confirmation**.

The Summary briefly goes over the main points of the discussion, the solution or **understanding** that has been reached between parties through the discussion and the commitments to **future action** made as a result. It should be specific, brief and clearly understandable. ('So what we've decided to do is...')

The Confirmation asks the other person to indicate their understanding of and agreement to the summary so that all parties have the same understanding of what has occurred. ('Is there anything I left out?' or 'Is that your understanding of what we have agreed?')

Fact Finding and Handling Poor Performance

Functional communication will be of use in every aspect of a manager's work. Particularly useful in the area of employee relations are similarly functional communication techniques for discovering the facts of a situation and for talking to team members about some aspect of unsatisfactory performance.

Fact Finding Techniques

Sound and complete information is a prerequisite for successful handling of grievances or complaints, or problems, or incidents that may call for disciplinary action - in fact, all those situations which directly or indirectly impinge on employee relations at the shopfloor level.

The **theme** and **cue** technique is used to open the discussion by stating simply the area of investigation, the information needed and its importance, followed by an open question that invites the other person to tell all they feel is relevant.

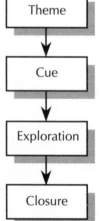

fig 11.6

Exploration of the **What, Who, When, Where** and **Why** of the situation follows next.

Who is involved? Were there witnesses and if so, who? Were managers involved and if so who? Who is the staff representative?

What actually happened? There may be several versions of an event, which will need exploration to get the true picture

Where precisely did the incident take place?

When precisely did the incident happen?

Why did the incident occur? Again, different people may have different explanations or perceptions of the reasons for what happened which will need investigation before forming any conclusions

Then as with all discussions a brief summary and confirmation of agreement and any commitments is used to close it.

Handling Poor Performance

Managers will sometimes have to deal with poor work habits or other problems which if left unchecked might lead later to more serious difficulties which could require disciplinary action. It's vital that these problems are dealt with before they affect the general morale of a team. It is also vital for good employee relations that they are handled in the right way.

ACTION POINT 26

We looked earlier at work improvement discussions in Chapter 6 on counselling. Note down what you recall of the essential points about tackling such a discussion.

Look back to Chapter 6 to check your answers.

ACTION POINT 27

You hold regular team meetings at 9.00am on Monday mornings when you brief your team members on the week's workload, deadlines and priorities. Roy is consistently late for these meetings and other team members have voiced their discontent about this. You ask Roy to come into your office.

Write down your suggestions for

1   A **Theme** opener (of not more than 2 sentences) establishing the subject of the meetings, so that the individual knows there is a problem

2   An open question **Cue** seeking a solution to the problem from the team member

3   A brief summery of the structure or outline of how you would develop the discussion after that point

CHAPTER SUMMARY

Having completed this chapter, you should now

■   understand the importance of effective communication in creating effective performance

■   have the ability to raise important discussions without setting up hostile or defensive reactions

If you are uncertain about any of these areas, look back and re-read the relevant parts of the text.

12 THE FORMAL AND LEGAL CONTEXTS

Although the manager is likely to make every effort to resolve employee relations problems positively in an informal way, it is clearly vital for them to understand the formal employee relations machinery and the legal framework they operate within. Decisions about treating a particular problem formally or informally may be affected by company policy or trades union agreements, or by the legal implications of a particular action; and informal actions when handling a situation in a particular way may, consciously or unconsciously, later affect any formal action that is taken with regard to it.

Following the right procedures according to national and local agreements with unions is not only important from the legal or formal point of view, however. Where there are grievances or problems to be dealt with, agreed procedures help to ensure full investigation, equality and fairness of treatment, sound decisions, and effective action and follow up. They also mean that people know how their grievance or problem or disciplinary hearing will be dealt with, and give them confidence that it will receive proper attention. So the manager's understanding of the formal context, knowledge of local agreements and procedures, and ability to work within these effectively will have an important effect on the team's confidence and trust, and thus on the climate of employee relations within the team.

The Industrial Relations Machinery Framework

The formal industrial relations machinery will involve agreements, procedures and bodies set up and maintained for

■ settlement by negotiation of terms and conditions of employment of persons employed by the company or organisation, sometimes with provision for reference to arbitration in default of settlement through the agreed procedures

■ consultation and discussion of matters affecting such things as the safety, health and welfare of persons employed by the organisation, and other matters of mutual interest

Terms and conditions of employment is, of course, a way of describing in brief such items as pay, pensions, working hours, holidays and periods of notice - which are referred to in a person's contract of employment.

ACTION POINT 28

What is the essential distinction between these two functions?

Negotiation

Negotiation involves **bargaining**. It is also one means of deciding how the money available in an organisation or business enterprise should be distributed - with negotiations on holidays and working hours being translated into money terms for this purpose. The aim of negotiation is to achieve an acceptable balance and compromise between the various requirements. Such agreements are generally not legally binding, but they are usually 'binding in honour'.

Consultation

In a consultative committee management and staff representatives exchange ideas in **discussion** of problems or matters of mutual concern. A consultative committee does not strictly speaking make decisions or reach agreements which are binding on its members. On the other hand it is more than simply a 'talking shop'. It can collectively **recommend** lines of action to appropriate members of management or staff.

Representation

Representation in negotiating matters is generally by elected or appointed trades union representatives on the employees side and by senior personnel and other management representatives on the employers side. According to the kind of matters under negotiation and the agreements under which they operate, the machinery may involve negotiations at local plant level or at an area or national level.

On consultative committees, employee representatives may be nominated or elected staff or union people, according to the agreed composition of the bodies. In companies where union representation is not present or recognised, a staff side body which does not have the recognised legal status of a trade union is likely to be involved in discussions and negotiations.

Policy, Rules, Conditions and Procedures Agreements

As a result of negotiations on conditions of service and discussion on other matters of mutual interest, in a company or organisation of any size, a body of agreed conditions and procedures will have grown up (and will be changing continually) on every aspect of work and the workplace - this will include also statements of company policy and company regulations about employee obligations and entitlements. It will include such things as agreed disciplinary and grievance procedures, how changes in working practices are to be agreed and implemented, local reward systems and so on - all of which the manager will need to know about and take account of in their everyday duties.

The Legal Framework

As well as negotiated or consultative agreements, the manager must know the legal framework of employment and its impact on the workplace. **Employment law**, conferring both rights and obligations, covers almost every aspect of working life - from the rights in defined circumstances to written Contracts of Employment, time off for union duties, redundancy payments, maternity leave etc to the obligations to meet certain Health and Safety standards, not to discriminate at work on grounds of sex or race and so on.

Some of the most important Acts of Parliament containing such provisions are

The Employment Acts of 1980 and 1982

The Employment Protection (Consolidation) Act 1978

The Equal Pay Act 1970 (Amended 1983)

The Sex Discrimination Act 1975

The Race Relations Act 1976

The Health and Safety at Work Act 1974

There are also **Codes of Practice** in many of these areas issued by such bodies as ACAS, the Department of Employment and the Equal Opportunities Commission which set out 'good practice' to follow to promote good employer/employee relations and avoid unintentional breaches of the law where specific law applies. These legal provisions (and many of the provisions in the different Codes of Practice) are often embodied in company regulations and procedures documents for management and staff to follow.

Whilst managers may not be expected themselves to know every detail of this legal framework, it is important that they

■　　are aware of **how** the law applies and in **what areas**

■　　recognise that they have a responsibility to obtain necessary information and to keep that information up to date

Ignorance of the law is not a defence where the law is broken. Official guides to legislation which currently applies can be obtained from Employment Offices, DHSS Offices, Health and Safety Executive Offices and HMSO Government Bookshops. These set out the main provisions, but for more detailed information or advice about how an incident may be affected by the law, managers may need to **seek advice** from a personnel or employee relations specialist in the company.

In the Appendix to this text (the Legal Framework) you will find a summary of the main legal provisions (and exemptions) affecting the workplace, with details of where the legislation may be found for each area and any relevant Guide or Code of Practice that is available.

The Need to Know the Framework

Clearly the range of Employment Law and Codes of Practice is very broad and we cannot look in detail at every area and every type of managerial problem where legal aspects or industrial agreements have to be considered. But to indicate the importance of **an awareness** of these dimensions we will look briefly at some examples.

ACTION POINT 29

1   A female member of staff in your workplace complains to you as manager that she is 'not being treated fairly' by other members of staff.

What would you need to find out to decide what action if any, to take?

2   In recruiting for various skilled jobs which require the understanding of fairly complex written instructions and procedures, your company includes in the selection tests a fairly sophisticated language test as one test of suitability. In recruiting for unskilled jobs which require an understanding of only very basic job and safety instructions they include the same language test which is unrelated to the job and it has the effect of 'failing' most of the non-indigenous applicants who ask to be considered.

You come across this practice on moving into the Personnel section and are worried that it may be unfair. What do you need to know to decide if any action is needed?

In the first case you will certainly need to find out fully from the person what has happened that they see as unfair treatment. You may subsequently need to see other people to check the facts. But you will probably be aware in general terms, that there could be **legal implications** in such a situation - that it is not lawful to treat people unfairly or unequally on grounds, for example, of sex or race. So you will need to know

■   what 'unfairness' or unequal treatment means in the legal sense

■   what areas are covered by the law and what the provisions are

■   what company policy and procedures are regarding the handling of such complaints

In the second case you will need to know the same things and in particular the legal provisions relating to **indirect** discrimination on grounds of racial or ethnic origin which are set out in the part of the Appendix which deals with racial discrimination.

ACTION POINT 30

1   Can you think of occasions outside the field of Equal Opportunities where ignorance of the legal framework could have legal consequence for a company at a later stage?

2   List some of the problems which might arise where supervisors or managers are insufficiently aware of how employment and other legislation affects the workplace.

Unless a manager knows the areas covered by legislation and their main provisions, and appreciates their practical effect in the workplace, they will not be properly equipped to

■ respect and positively promote the employment rights of their people

■ foresee potential problems where rights are or could be infringed

■ avoid the risk themselves of practices which are undesirable or unlawful

■ advise their people if any of their actions or procedures are undesirable practice or risk breaching the law

■ interpret and communicate company policies on such matters effectively to their people

■ use their skills and knowledge to prevent employee relations problems and even unlawful situations developing

In addition they will not run the chance of creating discord and bad relations by thoughtlessly unfair treatment or failing to respect the employment rights of their people, and they will avoid the consequences of

■ failure to take action to ensure compliance with legal obligations which may have serious repercussions for both the company and individuals. In many circumstances, unless an employer, manager has taken 'all reasonable practical steps' to prevent unlawful actions by staff, **they and the company may be liable also** for the actions (or failure to act) of employees

■ failure to follow agreed or recommended procedures which may also have serious consequences for a company (in grievance or disciplinary cases, for example, or in the field of Health and Safety)

Interpreting and Communicating Policy

The potential damage of ignorant or ill-judged actions by manager or team members in these areas - in team morale and performance or in terms of company and personnel liabilities - make it vitally important also that company regulations, policies and procedures are **clearly interpreted** and **specifically communicated** to people by the manager, so that they are in no doubt about their rights and obligations in any situation.

Of course, simply communicating rights and keeping within the law will not in themselves enhance the employee relations climate. The **manner** in which such knowledge is communicated and used will also determine how people respond and what kind of climate is established. If knowledge of law and policy is used positively to ensure people avoid problems and receive their rights, it will not only avoid the danger of breaking the law, but will create the kind of atmosphere in which good industrial relations flourish.

ACTION POINT 31

Read over the following case study and answer the questions that follow.

You will find it helpful before writing your answer to Question 1 to read over the Section on 'Sex Discrimination' in the Appendix - The Legal Framework.

Jenny Fortune's Transfer

Brian Parker is the Superintendent Supervisor of an engineering workshop, discussing the filling of a vacancy in the section supervised by Bill Swales, who has run a section for almost 20 years and is both experienced and efficient in his work.

A young engineer, Jenny Fortune, in another workshop has expressed an interest in doing a 2 week training course to transfer into this vacancy and no one else so far has expressed any interest in it. Brian is talking to her present Superintendent, John Tebbutt, about the position. Tebbutt says that her immediate supervisor says she is a good worker and in every way suitable, but that he personally is reluctant to agree to the transfer.

He says, 'I've heard from a colleague who knows Bill Swales that it's not a good idea. Swales is always saying an engineering shop is no place for women - 'It's not a bloody hairdressing salon', you know the sort of thing - and they won't get him having girls in his section. It would be just asking for trouble to transfer her. So I shall tell Jenny we can't afford to release her just at the moment, but that I'll make absolutely sure she gets the first vacancy in the future. And you'd better try and get that one filled quickly, Brian, because she'll probably come back to me on it, I imagine.'

Brian Parker is worried about whether this 'is fair' on Jenny and decides to talk to his manager before looking for anyone able to fill the vacancy.

Imagine you are the Engineering Shops manager and this situation comes to your attention.

1 Explain briefly how an awareness of the legal framework and of any staff regulations would be both necessary and helpful in dealing with the situation outlined above

2 Explain briefly how you would advise Brian Parker to tackle the situation, endeavouring to make sure no employee is treated unfairly, to avoid the dangers of any unlawful or undesirable action, to maintain harmonious employee relations within the teams as far as possible and to avoid future problems of a similar kind.

The knowledge of the legal framework and of any Staff Regulations would

(a)   enable you to decide whether John Tebbutt's proposal was an acceptable one under the staff regulations and whether it had any adverse legal implications.

(In fact, you will probably have realised that John Tebbutt's suggestion, while obviously well meant, would mean that Jenny Fortune was being refused both training and a job opportunity - even if temporarily - not because of her ability or qualifications for the job, but solely because she is a woman. If acted on, John Tebbutt's suggestions would mean that both he and Brian Parker had broken the law and of course any staff regulations which forbid discrimination. Provided you as a manager had drawn your staff's attention to the regulations and taken all reasonable, practical steps to ensure that equal treatment prevailed in your section, then the company and you as manager would not be liable; but in companies which do not take 'all reasonable practical steps' to ensure equal treatment, there would also be a legal liability on the employer and management for the employee's actions.)

(b)   enable you to explain to the supervisors why the action was not acceptable, as well as being necessary background to any discussion with Bill Swales about the transfer, and about Jenny Fortune's future position in his section

As manager you would need to point out to both superintendent supervisors that, however worthy the motives, John Tebbutt's suggestion is in practice unequal treatment on the basis of Jenny's sex and that what must be monitored (and tackled if necessary) would be any suggestion of discrimination against her when she moves into Bill Swales' section.

A decision on whether to talk to Bill Swales at this stage (other than letting him know about the impending transfer in the normal way) would depend very much on your own and Brian Parker's knowledge of Bill Swales and relationships with him. Certainly it would be unwise and unjustifiable to say anything which assumes his opposition or intention to discriminate, since the only indication you presently have of his attitude is hearsay and people do not by any means always behave as they say they are going to!

You may well judge it beneficial to circulate a reminder to all staff about the general provisions of Equal Opportunities regulations, without necessarily linking this directly to Jenny's transfer.

The best approach may be for Brian Parker to tell him about Jenny in the normal way, to give praise for the way he has helped new people to settle into the team in the past, and to indicate his own high expectations of the help and co-operation Bill will give to Jenny when she joins the team.

If anything arose in the discussion to suggest a potential problem, then Brian Parker would need to point out positively the staff regulations and law, and gain Bill Swales' acceptance of the need to conform to these.

By modelling the right attitude and expecting the best from Bill Swales, Brian may well find the anticipated 'problem' does not arise. If his informal monitoring of the situation shows this had not worked, however, he must be prepared to talk to Bill Swales about the position and, pointing out to him the possible breaches of the law and Staff Regulations, get from him suggestions and commitments about how he will behave in future to avoid these dangers. At this stage Brian will also have to decide upon the degree of formality or informality to use and this will probably depend upon such factors as

■ what has happened to make him believe Bill Swales is not treating Jenny Porter 'equally'?

■ what facts any investigation of this brings to light (whether there is clear evidence of a breach of the Staff Regs or Sex Discrimination Act, for example)?

■ his judgement as to whether the matter can be best resolved informally at this stage, or whether it requires some kind of formal record and warning, or whether company procedures demand that it be put on a formal footing and referred higher at this stage?

In any event he would be wise to make an informal record if any such discussions proved necessary with Bill Swales , and he should be ready to call you in if it becomes appropriate.

CHAPTER SUMMARY

Having completed this chapter, you should now

■ realise the importance of understanding the formal employee relations machinery and the legal framework they operate within

■ know which Acts and Codes of Practices to read and know where to obtain them

If you are uncertain about any of these areas, look back and re-read the relevant parts of the text.

13 DISCIPLINARY AND GRIEVANCE ISSUES AND PROCEDURES

As well as the legal rights and obligations which managers must be aware of (for both themselves and their people), they will need to be familiar with a whole range of agreed procedures and practices which form the local employer/employee relations background. And in terms of managing employee relations effectively, none of these will be more important than their knowledge and handling of grievance and disciplinary procedures.

Though operating at most times within the informal system, they will be well aware that something which starts out apparently as a minor grievance can rapidly escalate into something more serious if it is not handled skilfully, promptly and properly. And they will also need to assess when a transition from the informal to the formal systems is appropriate in handling both types of issue.

Disciplinary Matters

A sound formal disciplinary procedure will have certain essential elements

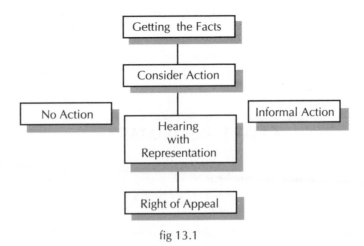

fig 13.1

Thorough Factual Investigation

Getting the facts accurately and fully is **always** relevant whether the problem appears to be minor or a more serious breach of company regulations

Consideration of Appropriate Action

It is important for managers

- to be sure they are acting within their authority and in accordance with agreed procedures

- to consider carefully all the circumstances, the gravity of the offence and what penalty is laid down by staff regulations or has previously been custom and practice in comparable circumstances.

A Hearing with Representation

It is a matter of natural justice that where something may go on an individual's record, the individual can have someone to speak for them if they wish - preferably someone who has experience of the procedures, and previous practice in such cases. Having a staff representative present should also help to ensure that the outcome is one which is acceptable and consistent with any management agreements.

A Right of Appeal

To guard against error or personal bias, a sound procedure enables an individual to have the right of appeal against a decision so that the incident or case can be looked at again.

Informal or Formal Action?

As noted above the first step in dealing with any potential disciplinary situation is to establish the facts by careful investigation, using the fact finding techniques we have just looked at in Chapter 9. At this stage a manager may judge that the incident is relatively minor and it will be counterproductive to deal with it formally, or that other special circumstances make a disciplinary type of interview undesirable.

Many problems exhibited at work may arise from a range of personal difficulties - emotional, domestic or health problems, alcoholism etc and it may be inappropriate to apply hard and fast procedures rigidly to them. A different approach may be needed, using the counselling skills looked at earlier to explore the situation and provide a supportive environment for the individual to discuss the problem. Such interviews should be conducted with an understanding of complete confidentiality and handled carefully since problems of this kind are likely to be highly emotional issues.

ACTION POINT 32

Bill Simpson has been a department supervisor for nearly ten years and has gathered a good team of men. He is now within three years of retirement and is naturally not quite as energetic as at one time -however, John Wood the manager has had no cause to complain about the overall efficiency of the department.

Simpson has three supervisors reporting to him and six months ago a vacancy arose in one of these positions. Among those who applied for the job were Harry Bishop and Ted Jackson, both tradesmen in the department. At that time Harry Bishop was 50 and had worked for the organisation for 22 years, spending the last 10 years in this department. He was regarded as a reliable tradesman who could be quick tempered and argumentative at times. On the whole though his record had been good.

Ted Jackson is a much younger man, about 35, who had joined the organisation only five years ago. He had shown himself to be a first class tradesman. In addition he was seen as something of a go-getter and his supervisors had always reported favourably on his work and initiative. It was known that he was friendly with Bill Simpson and that they often met in the club near their homes for a drink and a game of snooker.

Four men, including Bishop and Jackson, were on the final selection interview list and the job was ultimately offered to Ted Jackson.

In his first few months Ted Jackson settled into his job well and Bill Simpson was able to report to Wood that the was very satisfied with his progress. Ted was determined to show that his part of the department could do even better. He had noticed that several men, including harry Bishop, were at times slow to resume work after breaks and weren't working as conscientiously as he thought they could.

Yesterday morning Bill Simpson was away from work and Ted Jackson deputised for him in a meeting with the Human resources Manager. On his way back to the office he was passing the canteen when he saw Harry Bishop about to go in. As it was still more than ten minutes before lunch time he stopped Harry and asked why he was there at that time.

Harry replied that there was never any decent food available if you didn't get into the canteen quickly and that he was sick of men from other departments getting in first. Ted Jackson pointed out the time and said that Harry had better get back to the job until it was time to go for his break. At this Harry started arguing, lost his temper and became personally abusive. He pointed out men from other departments going into the canteen early. While this was going on the lunch signal went and Ted tried to calm Harry down, but without success. He left him, saying that he would be reporting the incident to Bill Simpson and Harry would hear more about this later.

Ted Jackson went back to the office and when Bill Simpson came in at 1.30pm he reported Harry Bishop adding that he intended to reprimand him formally. Bill Simpson asked if Ted Jackson would see him at 12.15pm in order to discuss the incident further. Shortly afterwards Harry Bishop came back from the canteen and seeing Bill Simpson in his office went in and apologised for losing his temper. He asked Bill to overlook the incident this time.

1   How in your view should Ted Jackson have handled the situation?

2   What should Bill Simpson do now?

Compare your ideas with what follows.

To avoid arousing emotions and to deal effectively with the situation, Ted should have maintained a cool and controlled approach and not become embroiled in an argument, by rushing into the situation without real thought in the heat of the moment and by allowing his own (laudable) wish for his department to perform 'even better' to affect his judgement.

He is acting as Simpson's deputy and therefore he should sort out the problem at grass roots. This may not always be possible - sometimes it must go upwards - but in this case, better handling should have been able to resolve the situation positively, rather than worsening it.

Clearly something needs to be done about Harry Bishop's action - once ignored, such a thing could easily become practice and difficult to correct. But it ought to be able to be handled informally at this stage - and it could provide an opportunity to improve his position with Harry Bishop, who may well feel resentment over the promotion of someone younger and with fewer years of service than himself.

If he really felt it necessary to go into the situation there and then, Ted might have asked Harry what he thought could be done to resolve the problem so that he would not need in future to stop work more than ten minutes early.

Instead of trying to use his authority to order Harry Bishop back to work when there was only a few minutes at most to the lunch break and he could not really check out the reasons given, it might have been better for Ted to have tried to find out more about the canteen problem (and preferably to have seen what he could have done to resolve it by talking to Bill Simpson and anyone else he needed to) before seeing Harry Bishop again later.

He should have checked out the facts, once Harry had answered his enquiry, and found out what could be done to overcome the problem, he could explain what was proposed and get his agreement that this solution would avoid any need to stop work early in the future. Being seen to listen and to act upon the problem would have gained him far more than an assertion of authority which would create only ill feeling and resentment if the grounds for the grievance were genuine.

Bill Simpson needs to see Ted Jackson to put him right in a supportive way on how he could have handled the situation more positively and how, by focusing on the problem, he could have avoided falling into the trap of becoming embroiled in a personal dispute. This would involve pointing out the positive long term results of being seen to listen and try to support staff with genuine grievances and not to react precipitately, without considered investigation, if corrective action was needed with a team member. He should stress the need to be consistent and fair and to act only after a considered assessment of the facts that are discovered, as well as due consideration of such things as customs and practice and known regulations.

Bill Simpson should also have indicated his own readiness to receive feedback and give support over any problems of this kind, since it is here at the grass roots that good industrial relations are most critically fostered or damaged. All this should be done privately of course.

Within the book, however, Simpson needs to support Jackson and speak to Bishop (again in private) about losing his temper, swearing and getting personal.

It would probably not be a good idea, however, for Simpson and Jackson both to see Bishop together. It is more likely that Bishop would be prepared to apologise informally later to Ted Jackson if he had the chance to express his view of the situation and feelings to Bill Simpson privately. Being asked to apologise formally in front of Bill Simpson and in a two-against-one situation might well exacerbate the situation by making Harry Bishop feel he has to justify himself and attack Ted Bishop's attitude.

Bill Simpson may also need to work on the canteen problem if it is something which is outside Ted Jackson's scope for action.

Following the Formal Procedures

Although employee relations can be managed very effectively within the informal system, there will be times when staff behaviour involves a more serious breach of the rules or affects other people's work performance and formal action is necessary. But as always formal action should only be set in train after a **thorough investigation** to establish the facts of the situation, obtaining information about and perceptions of the incident or problem from **all** those who have knowledge of it. No action should be decided upon, however, until the individual concerned, with his or her staff representative, has been given an opportunity to discuss the matter fully.

Planning the Interview

It is important to think through and plan such a meeting thoroughly. Nothing could be worse for employee relations or for the team's trust in their manager, than for a formal meeting to be set up which is shown to be unjustified because there has not been a proper investigation of aspects of the incident or problem, or of all the relevant company regulations, local agreements and 'custom and practice' in that area.

The manager should

- consider **WHAT** the meeting is about and check carefully all their facts

  When did the incident occur (dates, days, times, was it during a shift?)

  Where did it happen?

  Who was involved?

- think about **WHY** the meeting is necessary (be certain of the rules surrounding the incident)

- consider **WHO** should be at the meeting

  The individual involved?

  The staff representative? Others?

- think carefully about **WHERE** to hold the meeting. Talking to someone in front of their colleagues will cause resentment

- consider **WHEN** the meeting should take place. Rushing into an interview is unwise. People's availability and disruption to work are other factors to consider

Opening, Conducting and Closing the Interview

ACTION POINT 33

Compare these two ways of starting an interview. Write down briefly what reaction you think each would create in the team member.

1   The manager angrily confronts John in front of his workmates: 'Look here, John - nobody's getting any work done in your group because you are constantly going off to play in the cards syndicate. Now don't deny it . . . I've had enough - you're getting a written warning - now get on with the job . . .'

2   The manger finds a quite office and calls John in: 'Sit down John . . I've heard there is a cards syndicate going on in work time that is affecting the department's work as a whole. I've checked it out and it seems you're involved, so I've called you in so that we can have a chat about it. If it's the case, you know it's against company regulations, so I'd like to hear what you have to say about it . . .'

It is important that the individual should know straight away why they have been called to an interview, but the issue should be presented clearly **without any prejudgement** of it.

The first approach is aggressive and clearly assumes guilt. Even if correct, John is likely to feel humiliated and angry rather than inclined to amend. The second approach, however, is firm but not aggressive and encourages him to talk about the situation, showing that the manager hasn't already decided the case.

It is important **during the interview** to try to keep a dispassionate and calm atmosphere in which the issue can be dealt with fairly and with as little negative feeling and outcome as possible. It will help if the manager

- concentrates on the problem behaviour itself in a factual manner, not on the person involved

- sets out the reasons for the interview, the case, the supporting evidence and the way in which it breaks company rules as factually and directly as possible

- gives the individual and their staff representative a proper opportunity to give their case with any relevant supporting evidence

At **closure of the meeting** the manager needs to

- summarise what has taken place and make sure it is agreed by those involved

- state the decisions and any action to be taken clearly, and get confirmation these are understood

- make a written record and inform personnel or other appropriate people of the decision

---

ACTION POINT 34

Consider how this manager ends his interview with John and note down what you think is wrong with this approach.

'Right, John - I'm going to get to the bottom of this and I can see it will end up with you being disciplined. I'm warning you - this is the last time. That's my final decision - now get out of here....'

You will have noticed a number of problems here.

Exactly what decision has been made? Has John been given a warning or not? Is the matter to be taken up at a higher level? What action has been taken? Has the staff representative been involved? Is he or she going to be?

It will not be clear to John and could well be a source of dispute later if not cleared up.

Now consider the following account of ending the interview.

ACTION POINT 35

Manager: OK, John - let's sum up. You admit that on four separate occasions you were away from your work playing cards - and we've got the dates here. You also know that's against the regulations. Do you agree?

John: Yes

Staff Rep: Agreed

Manager: You understand that under the agreed procedure, I can give you a formal warning and that's what I intend to do. Do you accept that, John? You can, of course, appeal to the Managing Director, if you feel that's unreasonable..

John: No, no. Its fair enough

Staff Rep: It seems consistent with what's happened in similar cases

Manager: OK, John this is a final reprimand which will be confirmed by me. It will stay on your record for 6 months and, if there are no more problems, after that we'll wipe the slate clean. Do you have any questions... ?

Note down the ways in which this is an improvement on the previous ending.

You will have noticed that in this case

- the details of the case were summarised and confirmed as correct
- the decision was clear and not ambiguous
- both John and his staff representative were given the opportunity to comment
- the appropriate action was agreed by all concerned
- John was informed of his right to appeal, knew exactly what action was being taken and knows how long that action would remain on his record

The Possible Disciplinary Actions

As we noted earlier, disciplinary action must be appropriate to the seriousness of the incident, the circumstances involved and company policies and precedents.

Agreed company procedures will differ, but often an **oral warning** or **admonishment** will be regarded as informal and not be recorded on the individual's personal record. The manager may choose, however, to keep their own record of the details in case any formal action is required at a later stage. Whatever sort of verbal warning is used, however, the manager should always make it absolutely clear that a warning is being given.

Written warnings or reprimands should always be **recorded**. A written warning should explain quite clearly why it has been issued and say what will happen if there is no improvement.

Reprimands involving sanctions are more serious and will normally involve consultation (and perhaps a hearing of the case) at a higher than managerial level. Whatever the disciplinary measure involved, it must be within the authority of the person concerned to impose and it must fall within the company's agreed disciplinary rules.

It is important to ensure that procedures work fairly and effectively. However, occasionally the individual concerned may feel that they have not been dealt with properly. Consequently the procedure provides a right of appeal and, as we saw above, information about further action open to the staff member should be provided.

Grievance Procedures and Action

It is preferable, of course, to try to resolve any staff problems **before** the stage at which formal grievance procedures need to be used. This is not always possible, however.

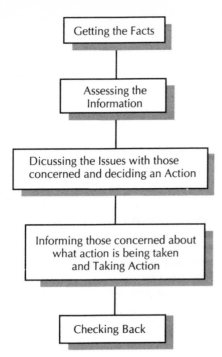

A good **grievance procedure** will include these stages

It should also allow provision for the grievance to be submitted to higher authority for arbitration or action, if the aggrieved person feels their problem has not been dealt with fairly or satisfactorily.

fig 13.2

Establishing the Facts - What the Grievance is About

However trivial an individual's grievance may appear to be to the manager, it will be important to that individual and must be checked out carefully to establish

- what actually happened?
- who was involved?
- when did the incident(s) or problem occur?
- why did the incident(s) or problem occur?
- do any rules or regulations cover the situation? If so, of what kind? (Company regulations? Custom and practice? Legal regulations?)

Information about the grievance should be written down while the facts are still fresh and the accuracy of any comments or statements made by individuals should be checked wherever possible.

Assessing the Information and Finding a Solution

It is vital that no judgement is made yet. If it appears the grievance can be resolved at this stage to the staff member's satisfaction, then the manager can (with the individual's involvement) consider what action can be taken (personally, or with others) to do this - for example, making necessary improvements in the working environment, or resources available to the staff member, if these are the source of the grievance.

Discussion of Proposed Action with the Individual

Any proposals should be recorded and talked carefully through with the individual concerned, seeking their views and suggestions. If the staff member thinks the proposals will resolve the grievance, then action should be taken as soon as possible, a written record made and follow up action arranged to check for a successful outcome.

If, however, the staff member does **not** find the suggested solution acceptable, the manager should explain how they can appeal or take the matter further and then, where necessary, inform the person(s) who will deal with the next level of the grievance procedure.

Being Aware of the Local Context

We have dealt earlier with the need for the manager to be aware of the legal background and the agreed employee relations procedures and practices within an organisation. We also mentioned 'local custom and practice' as an important part of 'the local context', as well as the relevant regulations and procedures. It will be within this 'local context' that the manager decides what action is appropriate in any disciplinary or grievance situation and it can be particularly relevant in the transition area between informal and formal action. To try to assess the complexity of issues which will make up the local context for a manager, look at the following situation.

ACTION POINT 36

Consider the following 'grievance' situation which, if left, could develop into a possible disciplinary matter.

A problem has developed in a computer room where fourteen staff work. The atmosphere is informal and the staff, who generally get on well together, find that they have to depend on each other to finish jobs that are required urgently, such as mounting tapes or discs for batch operations. Jane has been a member of the team for two years. Although quite competent in her work, Jane is not very popular with her colleagues. No one is willing to state what specifically is the problem. Among other remarks made in the office in the past have been: 'snooty', 'moody', 'temperamental', 'superior'.

Ever since she came into the department, Jane's frequent lateness and casual absenteeism from work have been a source of friction with other staff. Her Production Manager has tried from time to time to end this in an informal fashion, but Jane's record has become worse lately. Last week four of Jane's colleagues complained to the manager that she is never there when needed. The Production Manager has decided to interview Jane.

If you were the Production Manager dealing with this, what key contextual or other points would you need to know (or to find out) regarding

1   Local absence factors, policy and procedures that would affect your handling of the situation.

2   The specific case of Jane in the computer room?

The sort of absence factors, policies and procedures that a manager should know about as background to considering any situation like this would include

(a) knowing what injuries or illness, if any, might be sustained in the work area and any possible relationship between absence and Health and Safety factors

(b) awareness of what counselling or medical help may be available to help people improve health and attendance (Medical, Welfare, Human Resources etc)

(c) knowing how many days absence are acceptable and where the dividing line is at which local line management feel that absence is excessive

(d) full awareness of local procedures for dealing with absence (and when and how Medical, Welfare or Personnel departments may be involved in these); about when an individual should be spoken to for the first time, and the second etc; about what monitoring should be carried out and when to take further action if there is no improvement; about when and in what circumstances an unsatisfactory absence record becomes a possible disciplinary offence with line management and Human Resources being brought into the situation

In addition they need to be sure that they are prepared themselves so that they will handle any such situation effectively

(e) readiness to look into and tackle unacceptable absence records, using counselling skills where appropriate, but being firm on the need for improvement wherever required

(f) knowing:

how to fact find in handling absence records

how to assess and deal with any excuses that may be presented to them

what information may be available to them through the company medical section and what information may be available, with the person's consent through the local GP

how to make a decision that will deal with a situation without personalised accusations of malingering etc

In this particular case, as well as bearing in mind all the above points (and finding out any information relevant to them), the manager will clearly also need to know

(a) the full particulars (as far as they are known) of her absences, lateness etc, the reasons given for them and whether proper notification procedures were followed

(b)   specific details of what the four colleagues mean by 'she is never there when needed'

(c)   confirmation, if possible from records or other sources, that these complaints are objectively justified, not simply a result of Jane being seen as 'snooty', 'superior' etc.

ACTION POINT 37

Assuming that you possess all the necessary information about the local absence record procedures and policy (and have full details now of Jane's record), write down how you would conduct the initial interview to try to improve the situation and what steps you would have in mind for following up the interview.

Keeping Records in Grievance and Disciplinary Cases

It is very important that accurate records are kept if grievance or disciplinary matters take a more formal route, since these could finally be evidence for an industrial tribunal or even a civil court where there were possible legal aspects to the situation. And as formal processes may well follow earlier informal action, it is sensible to make notes, even when things are handled informally. Such notes may be needed at some future date either

■ for information - to confirm a fact or point of view

■ to write an accurate report of what happened regarding a particular individual or incident where further action is required or higher authority is brought into its handling

Incomplete or inaccurate records can themselves lead to disagreements and even disputes, as well as providing an unsound basis for any formal action that may result from a grievance or disciplinary matter.

In writing up any records or reports it is important to

■ be clear, concise and legible

■ be accurate, particularly regarding times, dates, places, names, what was said

■ avoid opinions and stick to facts

■ never write in the heat of the moment, even if immediate notes are made of a situation for the sake of accuracy

CHAPTER SUMMARY

Having completed this chapter, you should now

■ understand the skills involved in handling grievance and disciplinary procedures

■ have the ability to assess when a transition from the informal to the formal systems is required

■ realise the need to obtain accurate facts before action is taken

■ know how to carry out an investigative interview

If you are uncertain about any of these areas, look back and re-read the relevant parts of the text.

APPENDIX–THE LEGAL FRAMEWORK

The law gives protection and rights to employees in a number of areas. A quick reference summary of statutory employment rights and of the acts, codes and guides where information may be found is given here, followed by a section reviewing the basic provisions in more detail.

The abbreviations used in the Appendix refer to the Parliamentary Acts listed in the main text, or to codes and guides issued by the Advisory Conciliation and Arbitration Service (ACAS) or the Department of Employment (DE).

Summary of Statutory Employment Rights

Employment Rights	Statutory Sources/ Codes/Guides	Qualifying Period
1 Written Particulars of Terms of Employment	EP(C)A 1978 Sections 1-7 and 11 as amended by the 1982 Employment Act DE Booklet No 1	Full time - 13 weeks after commencement of employment Part time - one month after 5th anniversary of commencement of employment
2 Itemised Pay Statement	EP(C)A 1978 Sections 8-10 DE Booklet No 8	Full time - immediately Part time - after 5 years
3 Guarantee Payment	EP(C)A 1978 Sections 12-18 DE Booklet No 9	Full time - one month ending day before guarantee payment claimed Part time - after five years
4 Remuneration	EP(C)A 1978 Sections 19-22 DE Booklet No 5	Full time - one month ending day before payment claimed Part time - after five years
5 Trade Union Membership and Activities	EP(C)A 1978 Sections 23-26A Employment Acts 1980 and 1982 DE Booklets 7 and 13 DE Closed Shop Code of Practice	None

6 Time Off Work - Trade Union Duties and Activities	EP(C)A 1978 Sections 27 and 28 ACAS Code of Practice on Time Off	Full time - Immediately Part time - after five years
7 Time Off Work - Public Duties	EP(C)A 1978 Section 29	Full time - Immediately Part time - after five years
8 Time Off Work - Redundancy	EP(C)A 1978 Section 31 DE Booklet No 6	Full time - two years ending with effective date of termination of contract. Part time - after five years
9 Time Off Work - Ante Natal Care	EP(C)A 1978 Sections 31A Employment Acts 1980 and 1982 DE Booklet No 4	None
10 Time Off Work – Safety Representatives	Health and Safety At Work 1974 Section 2(4) HSAWA Regulations and Code of Practice (on Time Off for Training of Safety Representatives)	None, although Regulations state that as far as possible, a H&S representative should have been employed for at least two years or have two years experience in similar employment
11 Maternity Rights – Maternity pay and Right to Return to Work	EP(C)A 1978 Sections 33-48 DE Booklet No 8	Full time - two years at the beginning of 11th week before expected week of confinement Part time - five years
12 Minimum Notice of Termination of Employment	EP(C)A 1978 Section 49 DE Booklet No 14	Full time - minimum notice after one month's service and progressively thereafter Part time - after five years, then qualifies for five weeks notice
13 Written Statement of Reasons for Dismissal	EP(C)A 1978 Section 53 DE Booklet No 14	Full time - six months ending with effective termination of contract. Part time - after five years

14 Unfair Dismissal	EP(C)A 1978 Sections 54-80 TULRA 1974 and 1976 DE Booklet No 13 ACAS Code of Practice - Disciplinary Practice and Procedure	Full time - one year (two years if employed on or after 1/6/85). Two years in firm of less than 20 employees. Part time - five years
15 Redundancy Payments	EP(C)A 1978 Sections 81-102 DE Booklets Nos 2, 14 and 16	Full time - after two years, excluding any period of employment before 18 years old Part time - five years
16 Rights on Insolvency of Employer	EP(C)A 1978 Sections 121-127 DE Booklet No 3	None
17 Equal Pay	Equal Pay Act 1970 Section 31 Equal Pay (Amendment Regulations 1983)	None
18 Sex Discrimination	Sex Discrimination Act 1975 Equal Opportunities Commission Code of Practice 1985	None
19 Race Discrimination	Race Relations Act 1976 Commission for Racial Equality Code	None

Notes: All qualifying periods only apply to employees in continuous employment. A full-time employee is someone who works sixteen hours a week or more - a part time employee is someone who works less than 16 hours a week but no less than eight hours.

SOME FURTHER INFORMATION ON THE LEGAL PROVISIONS (AND CODES OF PRACTICE) RELEVANT FOR MANAGEMENT

1 Racial Discrimination

Details of the legislation relating to Racial Discrimination can be found in

- the Race Relations Act 1976
- the Commission for Racial Equality Guide and Draft Code
- there are two kinds of conduct that can constitute unlawful discrimination - direct and indirect discrimination.

Direct Discrimination

Treating a person less favourably than another on racial grounds. Racial grounds means on the grounds of colour, race, nationality, ethnic or national origins.

Indirect Discrimination

Applying to another persoi. a requirement or condition which is applied equally to persons not of the same racial group but which

(a)   is such that the proportion of persons of the racial group who can comply with it is considerably smaller than the proportion of persons not of that racial group and

(b)   cannot be justified and

(c)   is to the person's detriment because they cannot comply with it

An example of indirect discrimination might be if an employer were to impose a language test in recruitment procedures, which was not relevant to the work, but had the effect of excluding from consideration many people of non-indigenous origins.

Racial Discrimination in Employment

The Race Relations Acts cover unlawful discrimination in the fields of goods, public and private services, and housing, as well as in employment, but clearly it is the area of employment which is relevant here. The provisions cover both potential and actual employees.

(1)   Discrimination in Recruitment

This covers three main areas. It is unlawful to discriminate on racial grounds

- in any recruitment arrangements made to decide who should be offered a job
- in the recruitment terms on which employment is offered

■   by refusing or deliberately omitting to offer a job on racial grounds

(2)   Discrimination against Employees

This again covers three areas. It is unlawful to discriminate on racial grounds

■   in the contractual terms offered to employees - in pay, hours, holidays, shifts etc.

■   in a way in which access to opportunity is afforded, refused or deliberately omitted in promotion, transfer, training, and any other employee benefits, facilities or services

■   in dismissals or any other disadvantages to which employees may be subjected

(3)   Exceptions

The main exceptions relate to employment where being of a particular racial group is a Genuine Occupational Qualification (GOQ) for a job. In the following circumstances, for example

■   authenticity in drama, entertainment, modelling or restaurants

■   where the jobholder provides persons of that racial group with personal services promoting their welfare and those services can be provided most effectively by a person of that racial group. (This could apply for example, to the job of Health Visitor to women of Asian origin where for cultural and language reasons it might be difficult or impossible for a person of another racial group to provide that service effectively)

(4)   Other Unlawful Acts

It is also unlawful under the Race Relations Act

■   to publish or place for publication an advertisement which indicates (or might reasonably be understood to indicate) an intention to discriminate unlawfully (except where a GOQ applies)

■   for a person who is responsible for the work of another to instruct them to discriminate unlawfully

■   to induce a person to discriminate unlawfully by offering a benefit or threatening them with any disadvantage

■   to knowingly aid another person to discriminate unlawfully

An employer is also treated as liable for any discriminatory act done with or without his or her knowledge by any employee(s) in the course of their employment (in addition to the liability of the employee(s) themselves).

And it is also unlawful for a TU or an Employers Organisation to discriminate in the terms on which it admits a person to membership, or by refusing or deliberately omitting to accept a membership application.

(5)   General Exceptions

As well as the Genuine Occupational Qualifications exceptions, Parliament has also accepted the desirability of allowing some other exceptions for the purpose of overcoming the effects of racial disadvantage or past discrimination, and on grounds of national security

- Special Needs - an employer can discriminate to meet the needs of particular racial groups in regard to education, training and welfare eg. language training

- Discriminatory Training - this is permitted by employers in relation to a particular racial group for work in which, over the last 12 months, members of the group have either not been represented at all or have been under-represented in the company

  Discrimination is also permitted on racial grounds for the benefits of a person not usually resident in the UK in employment at a British establishment, where the purpose is to provide them with training in skills to be exercised wholly outside the UK

- Acts Safeguarding National Security - discrimination is not unlawful if done for the purpose of safeguarding National Security

2 Sex Discrimination

Details of the legislation on Sex Discrimination and its implications can be found in

- the Sex Discrimination Act 1986
- the Equal Opportunities Commission Code of Practice 1985
- the law states that it is unlawful to treat anyone less favourably on the grounds of their sex or marital status. Again unlawful discrimination can be of two kinds

Direct Discrimination

Treating a woman on the grounds of her sex less favourably than a man would be treated

Indirect Discrimination

Applying a requirement or condition which applies equally to all people but which means that

(a)   the proportion of members of one sex who can comply is considerably smaller than the proportion of members of the other and

(b)   it cannot be justified and

(c)   it is to the person's detriment because they cannot comply with it

Note that direct discrimination is also applicable in the case of married persons.

Discrimination in Employment

The main areas of employment where direct or indirect discrimination is unlawful include recruitment, employment opportunities and other detriments.

(1)   Recruitment

It is unlawful to discriminate on the grounds of sex or marital status

- in the arrangements being made for applicants for the job

- in the terms on which employment is offered

- by refusing or deliberately omitting to offer someone employment on the grounds of sex or marital status

(2)   Employment Opportunities

- it is unlawful to discriminate in the way in which access to opportunities is determined. This includes promotion, transfers, training and any other benefits or services

(3)   Detrimental Treatment in Employment

- it is unlawful to discriminate in the way in which employees of one sex are dismissed or subjected to any other detriment

(4)   Other Unlawful Acts

It is also unlawful under the Sex Discrimination Act 1986

- to publish an advertisement which indicates or might reasonably be understood to indicate an intention to discriminate unlawfully

- for a person who is responsible for the work of another to instruct them to discriminate unlawfully

- to induce or attempt to induce a person to discriminate unlawfully by offering a benefit or threatening to subject them to any detriment

(5)   Exceptions

However, there are certain exceptional circumstances where discrimination is not unlawful

- where the number of persons employed does not exceed 5
- where sex is regarded as a Genuine Occupational Qualification (GOQ)

For reasons, for example, of

- physiology eg. male models required
- decency or privacy eg. male or female toilet attendants

■ the nature or location of the establishment making it impracticable for the jobholder to live elsewhere than in the premises provided by the employer

■ where jobholders provide individuals with personal services promoting their welfare or education or similar personal services, and these services can most effectively be provided by members of one sex

■ where legal restrictions prevent the employment of women eg. mines

■ where the job involves performance of duties outside the UK in a country whose laws or customs militate against the employment of women eg. Saudi Arabia

■ certain discriminatory training is permitted by employers in relation to single sex training for work in which comparatively few members of that sex have previously been employed within the 12 months immediately preceding the training

Again employers are liable for the discriminatory acts of all their employees in the course of their employment, unless they can prove that they took such steps as were reasonably practicable to prevent their employees from discriminating.

Discrimination by Trade Unions is also unlawful - eg in criteria for admitting members to the union.

3 Maternity Rights

Information about employees Maternity Rights can be found in

■ the Employment Protection (Consolidation) Act 1978

■ the Employment Act 1980

■ the Department of Employment Leaflet No. 4

There are 4 basic rights for women in employment whether they are married or unmarried

■ right to time off with pay for ante-natal care

■ protection against unfair dismissal on grounds of pregnancy

■ right to maternity pay

■ right to return to work after confinement

(1)   Ante-natal Care

A pregnant employee who has been advised to attend for ante-natal care (by a doctor, midwife or health visitor) has the right to attend during working hours and to be paid for the time off, irrespective of her marital status and length of service. Except for the first occasion, the employee must have an appointment and the employer may ask to see confirmation of the appointment ie. the appointment card.

(2)   Unfair Dismissal

It is automatically unfair to dismiss a woman because she is pregnant or for a reason connected with her pregnancy; but in order to bring an unfair dismissal claim she still requires 2 years service. There are however two exceptions to this. Dismissal may be considered fair if, because of her pregnancy and at the time of the dismissal, the employee

(a)   is incapable of adequately doing the work she is employed to do

(b)   cannot do the work she is employed to do without contravention of the law eg. if she works with ionising materials or lead

However, even in the two exceptions given above, the dismissal is unfair if the employer has an alternative vacancy which would be suitable, but fails to offer it to her by the expiry of her employment contract.

(3)   Maternity Pay

In order to qualify the following conditions must be met

(a)   the person must be employed up to immediately before the start of the 11th week before the expected week of confinement (EWC)

(b)   she must have 2 years continuous service at the beginning of the 11th week before the EWC

(c)   if part-time, she works at least 16 hours per week, or has worked 8 hours per week for at least 5 years

(d)   she must be in possession of a medical certificate stating the EWC

(e)   she must inform her employer, in writing, 21 days before absence begins that she will be absent because of pregnancy

(4)   Return to work

An employee who leaves work to have a baby has the right to return to work in either the same job or, if that is not reasonably practicable, in a job which is suitable to her on terms and conditions 'not less favourable than those which would have applied if she had not been absent'.

To do this she must give her employer 21 days notice of her intention to return and in any event return within 29 weeks beginning with the actual week of confinement (this can be delayed by 4 weeks on either side).

An employer is entitled to check during a woman's absence whether she intends to return - this must be in writing and no earlier than 49 days after the start of the expected week of confinement. The woman then has 14 days in which to reply (the employer's letter must make this clear); if she does not comply with this request then she forfeits her legal right to return.

4 Dismissal

Information about the legislation and Codes of Practice relating to dismissals can be found in the

- Trade Union and Labour Relations Act(s) 1974 & 1976
- Employment Protection (Consolidation) Act 1978
- Employment Act(s) 1980 & 1982
- Department of Employment leaflet No. 13
- Department of Employment Guide
- ACAS Code of Practice - Disciplinary Practice and Procedure

(1)   The Definition of Dismissal

An employee is dismissed if

(a)   an employer dismisses him or her, with or without notice

(b)   he or she is employed under a fixed-term contract and it comes to an end

(c)   he or she resigns, but does so because the employer has acted in breach of contract ie. 'Constructive Dismissal'

(2)   Who can complain of Unfair Dismissal?

Every employee has the right not to be unfairly dismissed with the following exceptions

(a)   excluded classes: registered dockers; share fishermen; those ordinarily working outside the UK

(b)   those not continuously employed for 1 year (two years if employed on or after June 1st 1985)

(c)   those over normal retirement age for their organisation or over 60/65 if there is no normal retirement age

(d)   those working less than 16 hours per week (unless they have been employed continuously for at least 8 hours a week over at least 5 years)

(e)   employees of firms with fewer than 20 employees (unless they have completed 2 years continuous service)

(f)   employees on fixed term contracts of 1 year or more who have agreed in writing not to pursue a claim when the contract expires

(3)   Fair Dismissal

A dismissal can be fair if the reason (or the principal reason) falls within one of the following categories

- capability (skill, aptitude, health) or qualification
- conduct

- redundancy
- a breach of the employer's statutory duty if the employment were to continue
- some other substantial reason justifying the dismissal of an employee

If the fairness of a dismissal is disputed, an Industrial Tribunal decides whether or not the employer acted reasonably in all the circumstances. The test of fairness is as follows

> 'the determination of the question whether the dismissal was fair or unfair, having regard to the reason shown by the employer, shall depend on whether in the circumstances (including the size and administrative resources of the employer's undertaking) the employer acted reasonably or unreasonably in treating it as sufficient reason for dismissing the employee; and that question shall be determined in accordance with equity and the substantial merits of the case'
>
> (Employment Act 1980)

Where the fact of dismissal is not disputed, the evidential burden largely remains on the employer to show:

(a)   the reason for dismissal

(b)   that it falls into one of the 'fair' categories

(c)   that he or she acted reasonably in all the circumstances

In determining the question a tribunal may take into account any evidence of failure, on the part of the employer, to observe any relevant provision in a Code of Practice, or indeed in the employer's own regulations.

(4)   Inadmissible Reasons

It is automatically unfair to dismiss an employee for an 'inadmissible reason'. These are

- joining, or belonging to or taking part at an appropriate time in the activities of an independent union
- because of their race
- because of their sex

Unfair Dismissal claims on these grounds can be made regardless of the length of service with the employer, the employee's age or the hours per week worked.

(5)   Dismissal and Union Membership Agreements

In general dismissal for non-membership of a trade union in a closed shop situation is only fair

(a)   if the closed shop is approved by a ballot subject to the conditions laid down in the 1980 and 1982 Employment Acts and:

(b)   the individual does not fall into one of the special categories which legitimise non-membership of a union under a closed shop. It is worth nothing that there is no compulsion in law to hold a ballot and thereby gain approval for a closed shop - but only in so doing will an employer have a first line of defence against a closed shop unfair dismissal claim.

There is no qualifying period of service, qualifying hours per week or age limit for employees who wish to complain that they have been unfairly dismissed for non-membership of a trade union in a closed shop.

(6)   Dismissal and Industrial Action

If at the date of dismissal the employee was taking part in industrial action, an industrial tribunal will not have jurisdiction over the case unless it is shown that

■   not all of those employees taking part in the industrial action have been dismissed

■   or the employer had offered re-engagement to those taking part but the employee in question has not received a similar offer

(7)   Pressure on Employer to Dismiss

An employer cannot justify a decision to dismiss an employee on the grounds that pressure was exerted upon him by a trade union or other person calling, organising, procuring or financing industrial action, or threatening to do so, because the employee was not a member of a trade union. In such circumstances, however, the employer or the applicant may request an industrial tribunal to join that person exercising the pressure to be party to any proceedings for remedy - that is, they may also be liable if a dismissal is found to be unfair.

5 Rights to Time Off

Information about an employee's rights to time off may be found in the

■   Employment Protection (Consolidation) Act 1978

■   Department of Employment leaflet No 6 (Job hunting in Redundancy situation)

■   ACAS Code of Practice No. 3 (TU Duties & Activities) and No 12 (Public Duties)

■   Health & Safety At Work Act Regulations and Code of Practice

There are basically 5 rights to time off work. These relate to

■   TU duties

■   TU activities

■   public duties

■   job hunting and retraining

■   Health & Safety representative activities

(1)   TU Duties

An official (shop steward, representative) of a recognised trade union has the right to reasonable paid time off to carry out duties concerned with industrial relations between his or her employer or any associated employer and their employees, or to undergo training related to these duties.

To qualify as a duty, the representative must be doing something which is concerned with the industrial relations between the employer and the Trade Union.

(2)   TU Activities

A member of a recognised independent trade union has the right to reasonable time off without pay to participate in the activities of the union or to take part in activities at which he or she represents his trade union. The sorts of activities covered are: attending branch meetings, voting in a ballot, receiving feedback on pay negotiations etc.

(3)   Public Duties

A Justice of the Peace, Councillor, Statutory Tribunal member, Health Authority member, School or College Governor, or Water Authority member has the right to reasonable time off without pay to perform his or her public duties.

(4)   Job Hunting or Retraining

A person who has been given notice of dismissal because of redundancy and who would have at least 2 years' service on the effective date of termination has the right to reasonable paid time off from work to look for new employment or to make arrangements to retrain.

There is little guidance in the law as to how much time off should be permitted, but case law has established that it is sufficient for a person to request time off to look for alternative work.

(5)   Health & Safety Representative Activities

A person appointed as a Health and Safety representative by a recognised trade union has the right to paid time off to carry out their duties and they are also entitled to paid time off for training as a representative.

6 Trade Union Membership

Details of legislation and information about TU membership rights can be found in the

■   Trade Union and Labour Relations Act(s) 1974 & 1976

■   Employment Protection (Consolidation) Act 1978

■ Employment Act 1980

■ Employment Act 1982

■ Department of Employment leaflets 7 & 15

■ Department of Employment Code of Practice on Closed Shops

Every employee has the right not to be dismissed for

■ being a member of an independent trade union, or proposing to join one

■ taking part in its activities 'at an appropriate time'

■ refusing to join a union

Employees can also claim compensation if action short of dismissal is taken against them and they can prove they were victimised for any of the following reasons

■ to prevent them from exercising these rights

■ to penalise them for doing so

■ to compel them to join a union

(1)   Individual Rights under a UMA (Union Membership Agreement)

The 1980 and 1982 Employment Acts gave workers dismissed or victimised for refusing to join a union where a UMA exists substantial new rights.

The position is now that

■ dismissal or victimisation for not being a union member is unfair - except where a UMA exists, when dismissal or victimisation for not being a union member may be fair

However, the UMA is only valid if it has been approved by a ballot. A ballot is approved only if

(a)   for pre 1980 UMAs, either 80% of those entitled to vote, or 85% of those voting, agree to it

(b)   for post 1980 UMAs, 80% of those entitled to vote agree to it

The ballot must be secret, give a vote to all those within the class of employees to be covered, and not define the class by reference to union membership or objection to it.

However, even if the UMA is approved, victimisation or dismissal for refusing to join the union is still unfair if

■ the employee genuinely objects on the grounds of conscience or other deeply held personal conviction, or

■ the employee was there before the UMA took effect and since it took effect has never been a member of a union specified in the UMA

- in the case of UMAs taking effect after 15/8/80 the worker has not since the date of the ballot been a member

- the employee has a claim pending or has got a tribunal decision that she or he has been unreasonably excluded or expelled from the union

- the employee is covered by a professional code precluding industrial action and has refused to take action in breach of the code and has therefore been excluded or expelled from membership

So these provisions do not make the closed shop illegal and dismissal for failure to join a union under a UMA is not automatically unfair. However, an employer can only claim that such a dismissal was fair, if the UMA is approved and the individual does not fall into any of the categories above. This in practice makes it difficult to satisfy the conditions for a fair dismissal. There is no requirement in the law to hold ballots to approve UMAs and to date very few companies and trade unions have wanted to hold them.

7 Redundancy

Details of legislation and information on redundancy rights can be found in the

- Employment Protection Act 1975
- Employment Protection (Consolidation) Act 1978
- Department of Employment leaflet No 2
- Department of Employment Guide
- 1971 Code of Industrial Relations Practice paras 44-46

For someone's dismissal to be classified as redundancy, then the dismissal must be wholly or mainly attributable to one of the following

- the employer has ceased, or intends to cease, to carry on the business either at all or in the place where an employee is contracted to work or

- the requirements of that business for employees to carry out work of a particular kind, or for employees to carry out work of a particular kind either at all or in the place where they were contracted to work, have ceased or diminished or are expected to diminish

(1) Redundancy Payments

Not all employees losing their jobs for reasons of redundancy are eligible for redundancy payments. Those eligible are

- all employees who hold Contracts of Employment

- all employees with at least 2 years service
- all employees who are over 18 years of age

The following are not eligible

- the self employed
- those with less than 2 years service
- those who would reach 60/65 before the date of dismissal
- registered dock workers
- merchant seamen
- crown servants and employees in public office or in the NHS
- those on fixed term contracts for 2 or more years who have agreed in advance not to claim Redundancy Payments when the term expires
- off shore oil-rig workers
- apprentices on fixed term apprenticeships who are not employed at the end of their training

(2) Alternative Employment

Employees who refuse an offer of suitable alternative employment unreasonably (see Section 7(5) also), or who unreasonably terminate their employment after a 4 week trial period of alternative work, are not eligible for Redundancy Payments.

(3) Misconduct

In general an employee who is dismissed for misconduct is not entitled to Redundancy Payment. The 1978 Act applies this rule where the misconduct is serious enough to justify summary dismissal and where one of the following applies

(a) the employee is summarily dismissed or

(b) is dismissed with shorter notice than he or she is otherwise entitled to receive or

(c) is dismissed with full notice entitlement but receives a written statement from the employer recording the fact that the employer has the right to dismiss summarily

If the employee is dismissed for misconduct in any of the above 3 ways at a time when he or she is under notice of dismissal for redundancy, a tribunal has a discretion to award some or all of the redundancy payment he or she would otherwise have received.

(4) Strike Action

Employees who are already on strike when given their redundancy notices lose their entitlement to redundancy pay. Employees who strike when they have been given their redundancy notices do not lose their entitlements.

(5) Redundancy Procedure

(a) Consultation

Under the Employment Protection Act 1975, an employer has a statutory duty to consult trade union representatives when proposing any redundancy (The person consulted as the union representative must be authorised by the union to carry on collective bargaining).

In addition the employers must notify the Department of Employment if they propose to make 10 or more employees redundant at one establishment within a specified period.

The Act requires that consultation begin at the earliest opportunity. There are however 2 time limits on minimum periods of consultation

- if 10-99 employees are to be dismissed as redundant at one establishment over a period of 30 days or less - the minimum period should be 30 days before the first dismissal takes effect
- if 100 or more employees are involved at one establishment over a period of 90 days or less - the minimum period should be 90 days before the first dismissal takes effect

However there are certain important qualifications to these minima

- there is no requirement to start consultation before an employer is in a position to make a definite proposal
- special circumstances may make early consultation impossible or unwise

In consultation the employer is required to provide certain information in writing so that useful and constructive discussions may take place - in particular

- the reason for the proposed redundancy
- the number and occupation of those employees to be made redundant
- the total number of employees the employer has in each occupational group
- the way in which employees will be selected for redundancy
- how the redundancies will be carried out, taking into account any procedure agreements

(b) Selection

Employers may be liable to pay employees compensation for unfair dismissal if they

- select employees for redundancy in breach of agreed procedures or customary arrangements without special justification
- select employees for redundancy because of their TU membership or activities

Also employers may be liable if

- they fail to look for alternative work for redundant employees
- they fail to give employees reasonable advance warning or otherwise act unreasonably

(c) Alternative Work

As mentioned in (3) above there are certain provisions in relation to alternative work which might result in an employee being ineligible for redundancy payments

- if the employer makes an offer (whether in writing or not) before the ending of the employees' employment to renew his or her contract or to re-engage in alternative work and
- this offer is to take effect either immediately on the ending of the contract or after an interval of not more than 4 weeks

In relation to this offer

- either the new or renewed contract's terms and conditions, capacity and place do not differ from the previous contract, or the terms differ (wholly or in part) but the offer is one of suitable employment in relation to the employee
- the offer may relate to the same employer or an associated employer which, in effect, usually means another company within the same group

When an employee has accepted an offer of alternative employment he or she may 'test' it without prejudice to possible redundancy payments for up to 4 weeks - the 'trial period'.

(d) Time Off

An employee who is under notice of redundancy and who has 2 years service with the employer at the expiry of his notice, is entitled to paid time off during working hours to look for new work or to make arrangements for training for new work.

8 Equal Pay

The detailed conditions governing Equal Pay will be found in the legislation

- Equal Pay Act 1970
- Equal Pay (Amendment) Regulations 1983

The Equal Pay Act 1970 established a legal requirement of equal treatment for men and women in the same employment. It operates by treating every contract of employment which does not include what is called an 'equality clause' as if it did include such a clause. The equality clause is therefore an implied term of the contract of employment.

Unless an employer can prove that the variation between the women's pay and the man's pay is genuinely due to a material difference other than sex, then under the terms of the Equal Pay Act and subsequent regulations a woman can claim equal pay where she is employed on

- 'like work' - that is, work of the same or of a broadly similar nature or

- 'work rated as equivalent' under a job evaluation scheme or

- 'work of equal value' - that is, 'where a women is employed on work which is... in terms of the demands made on her (for instance, under such headings as effort, skill and decision) of equal value to that of a man in the same employment'

The Equal Pay Act and the regulations apply to men comparing themselves with appropriate women as well as to women comparing themselves with men. The requirement for equal treatment does not preclude special provisions for maternity, nor does it override previous legislation covering the employment of women (such as Factories Acts).